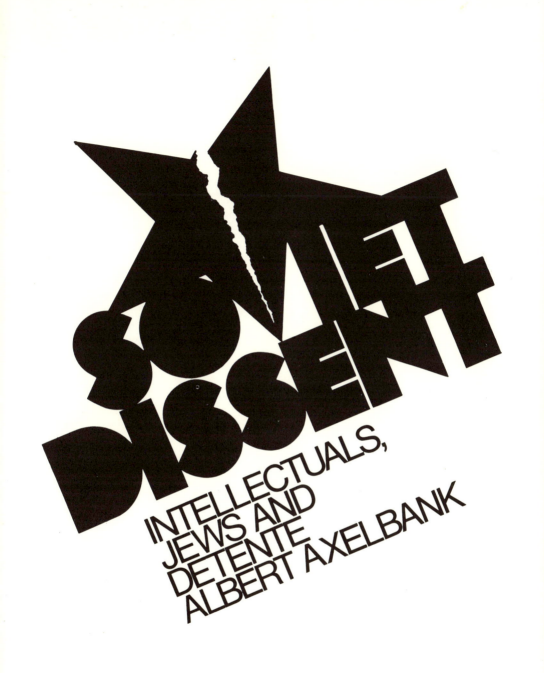

SOVIET DISSENT

INTELLECTUALS, JEWS AND DETENTE

ALBERT AXELBANK

Franklin Watts, Inc.
New York, 1975

TO NICOLAS DE B. F. TORRES

ALSO BY THE AUTHOR

Black Star Over Japan
Japan Destiny
Mongolia
Soul of the Gobi

Photos, courtesy *Newsweek*/Bernard Gotfryd (Yevtushenko, Nureyev)
Newsweek/Jay Axelbank (Sakharovs)

Library of Congress Cataloging in Publication Data

Axelbank, Albert.
    Soviet dissent; intellectuals, Jews, and détente.

    Bibliography: p.
    SUMMARY: Discusses contemporary dissent of intellec-
tuals, artists, and Jews in the USSR and examines a few
individual cases.
    1. Dissenters—Russia. 2. Russia—Intellectual Life—
1970–   3. Russia—Politics and government—1953–
4. Jews in Russia. [1. Dissenters—Russia. 2. Russia—Intellectual life. 3. Jews in Russia] I. Title.
DK274.A9   322.4'4'0947   74-13635
ISBN 0-531-02800-3

A WORD TO
THE READER

This book makes no attempt at encyclopedic treatment of Soviet dissent, which is a large subject with a multiplicity of experts. And often the experts don't agree. (As Charles Evans Hughes once said: "The history of scholarship is a record of disagreements.") The book seeks, rather, to convey some of the main currents of contemporary dissent in the USSR. In writing these pages the author has borne in mind something his old history teacher at the University of Wisconsin said: "Every question has two sides and both of them are wrong!" The reader should be cautioned that some of the questions raised in the following chapters have at least three sides to them.

A number of persons were kind enough to read the manuscript and make helpful suggestions. They include: Soviet affairs specialists Harrison E. Salisbury and Theodore Shabad, of the *New York Times,* and Jay Axelbank, formerly correspondent in Moscow for *Newsweek.* I also wish to thank my editor, Jane Steltenpohl. Responsibility for the views expressed is, of course, mine.

A. A.

TABLE OF
CONTENTS

1

THE AGONY
OF DISSENT

We must all toe the line, go forward together in orderly ranks—all artists as one—not under some kind of lash but in accordance with our conscience.

Statement by a Communist party official to
Aleksándr I. Solzhenitsyn

In a tense world they [the Soviet authorities] can't afford the luxury of excepting from total control a group of people who deal in critical ideas, moral judgments, imagination, beauty and words. They can't allow modern counterparts to Dostoyévsky, Tolstóy and Chékhov, or even to Gorky, who was Stalin's adviser on the arts.

Brooks Atkinson,
on Soviet criticism of Boris Pasternak

The collision of art with a social system is always a collision of freedom against repression, a combat of truth and lies, the struggle of life against deadening mechanism, and to put it into the language of religion—a fight between God and the Devil.

Mihajlo Mihajlov,
"The Artist as the Enemy," *New York Times,*
October 24, 1970

Between Christmas week 1973 and Valentine's Day 1974 a stunned international public beheld something new in Soviet social history: the ability of one man—Aleksándr I. Solzhenitsyn—to flout the Soviet regime from within. Actually, novelist Solzhenitsyn had been dipping his pen into inflammatory liquid for half a dozen years, and his criticisms were apt to be scorching. The climax in this long-standing feud, however, was the publication in the West, shortly before the new year, of *The Gulag Archipelago, 1918–1956*. This book was Solzhenitsyn's searing "documentary exposé" of Stalin's penal camps and, by implication, an indictment of the whole Soviet system. (Gulag is an acronym of the Russian for "State Administration of Labor Camps.") But a few months earlier, the author had sent to the Kremlin a 15,000-word letter which called for the abandonment of Communism and the splitting up of the Soviet Union. Outraged by the publication of *Gulag* and specifically attacking it, the Soviet Establishment used its strongest language against the author, calling him a renegade, slanderer, and fascist. Solzhenitsyn stood his ground and returned the fire.

The suspense ended on February 12 when the author was arrested, placed overnight in a prison cell, stripped of his Soviet citizenship (ordered by a decree of the Presidium of the Supreme Soviet) and deported the next day to West Germany. Solzhenitsyn had fully anticipated arrest, for he reportedly kept an overnight bag packed and ready next to his bed. Later—a departure from the rigidity of the past—the regime allowed the author's family to join him in his involuntary exile.

The Solzhenitsyn affair heightened international interest in the nature of Soviet dissent and its meaning for the USSR and the world. But although some observers interpreted dissent as a sign of Soviet decay, many others saw it as a natural result of the liberalization of that society since Stalin's death in 1953.[1]

Recently, American author Herbert Gold visited the Soviet Union and wrote a short essay entitled "The Dissenters Solzhenitsyn Left Behind." In it, Gold said that a change had occurred in that country since he had visited it nine years before. On his earlier visit he had noticed abject fear among the citizens toward the police. Now the people hardly gave thought to the police. But this was due, Gold said, not to any magnanimity of spirit in the regime but rather to what he called a "blitheness of desperation" among dissident intellectuals and Jews. It is difficult to assess the accuracy of Mr. Gold's judgment. Nevertheless, many experts are agreed that life in general is easier in the Soviet Union today than, say, in 1960. The regime exudes more self-confidence than in the days of Nikíta Khrushchév when the Kremlin had to boast of Soviet accomplishments on a daily basis. Moreover, this new self-confidence has permeated the general public so that many citizens are no longer so hesitant to speak their minds.

Some observers of Soviet politics assert that the relative tolerance of the Kremlin toward efforts of dissidents to publicize their cases overseas is one of the truly significant changes toward moderation since Stalin. In at least one case a dissident had the temerity to tell the KGB: "I demand that foreign correspondents be present!"

Literary dissent is widespread; few if any citizens are arrested anonymously anymore. Even the most perfervid anti-Communist admits that by comparison with Stalinist terror as described so chillingly in Solzhenitsyn's books, the Soviet regime has in recent years treated dissident writers and intellectuals with relative leniency. However, writers still must not undermine the basic socialist philosophy or the government's foreign policy. Thus, writers and intellectuals who protested the Soviet intervention in Czechoslovakia in 1968 were punished. Pavel Litvínov, a grandson of one of Stalin's foreign ministers and wartime ambassador to the United States, spent four years in Siberian exile for joining such a protest in Moscow's Red Square. (He had been warned to "stay out of politics.") In March 1974 Pavel Litvínov and his family left the Soviet Union for the West.

Also of significance is the fact that there is more flexibility nowadays in painting, sculpture, and music. If they choose, Soviet citizens can tune in their radios to the Voice of America. There is much less Soviet jamming (as of this writing), although the press and television remain, as before, the controlled organs of the state.

A world famous scientist and one of the most outspoken of the dissidents, Dr. Andréi D. Sakharov has cited five forms of contemporary "social protest" against the Soviet system: renewed religious feeling, nationalist activity in various Soviet republics, desire for emigration abroad, desire for cultural revivals among Russians, and widespread public drunkenness.[2]

Freedom as it is known in the West is not permitted. Indeed, a Communist party official in Leningrad has made this statement: "If you think that we will ever allow somebody to speak and write anything that comes into his head, then this will never be. We will never allow this." Thus "underground" newspapers are illegal. Some illegal publications have appeared in recent years but these samizdat, or "publish-it-yourself" materials, have been suppressed and those involved punished. Some incorrigible dissidents have been placed in mental homes, a devilish punishment against intellectuals that critics have called "psychiatric repression." [3] (A bit of wry humor making the rounds in Moscow in the early 1970s was that there were so many scholars and intellectuals confined in mental homes that these homes could easily be converted into universities! But the reality was no joking matter. For example, dissident Pyotr G. Grigorenko, a former Soviet army general, had spent five unbroken years in psychiatric wards. Grigorenko was arrested and ruled insane in 1969 after he zealously defended a group of Crimean Tatars who were charged with anti-Soviet acts. He had been arrested before that for so-called anti-Soviet behavior in the mid-1960s and been relieved of his officer's rank and dismissed from the Communist Party. He was released from the mental hospital in June 1974, and given a small pension, shortly before President Nixon's visit to Moscow.)

Late in 1973 two activists, Pyotr Yakír and Viktor Krásin were sentenced to three years in prison plus three more years in Siberian exile. They had been convicted of having published an illegal newsletter and having been paid agents for an anti-Soviet émigré group in Frankfort. But—times have changed—their sentences were later reduced to three years of exile not far from Moscow, because they had turned state's witness against themselves. Dissident historian Andréi Amalrik, author of *Will the USSR Survive Until 1984?*, also had a three-year prison sentence commuted to exile, and was given a post as senior laboratory assistant at a Siberian institute. In the Leningrad hijacking case tried in December 1970 against a number of Jews and others who had planned to hijack a Soviet airliner to escape abroad, two of the defendants were sentenced to death. However, after a spirited worldwide protest, the sentences were commuted to long prison terms. It is a sign of progress when a regime listens to world public opinion. If these cases had occurred in

Stalin's lifetime most of the defendants would not be breathing today.

Obviously the Kremlin does not want another Solzhenitsyn affair. But various external and internal factors—such as world tensions, the existence of émigré organizations, pressures for freedom of emigration, and demands by dissenters for greater freedom of expression inside the USSR—were almost a guarantee that dissidents would remain indefinitely on the Soviet stage.

Dissidents in the USSR are by no means a homogeneous entity. They include people on the borderline or virtually within the Establishment, such as Yevgény Yevtushenko and Andréi Voznesénsky, both poets, as well as those who are not only non-Marxist in thinking but also markedly anti-Soviet. Completely outside the mainstream of Soviet political culture are devout religionists, including some Baptists, Roman Catholics, and Russian Orthodox faithful. Some dissident Jews criticize the regime but wish to remain within it; others reject the Soviet system totally and wish to emigrate. Between the above extremes is a middle ground that includes historian Roy A. Medvédev, who considers himself a Marxist, favors Soviet-American détente, but is often a fierce critic of the Kremlin. For example, when *The Gulag Archipelago* was published, and scathingly attacked by the regime, nobody praised the work more highly than Medvédev.

Solzhenitsyn, like a number of other "free-thinking" Russians, is not only non-Communist but also anti-Soviet. He has totally rejected the Leninist revolution of 1917. However much political scientists disagree on the merits of different political systems, they are generally agreed that no revolutionary regime can remain revolutionary if it tolerates the diffusion of counterrevolutionary thought. Indeed, after Solzhenitsyn's forced exile, the world learned that the author actually preferred "the old Czarist days" to the modern industrial-technological state, whether under the Soviet or another banner.

Sovietologists compared the treatment of Solzhenitsyn to the deportation of Stalin's arch enemy, Leon Trotsky, in 1929. At that time, Trotsky was put aboard a Soviet steamship on the Black Sea and taken to Turkey. From there he went to Europe where one country after another rejected his plea for asylum. Finally, he was given refuge in Mexico where he was slain in 1940 by a Stalinist agent. Trotsky, incidentally, bitterly attacked Stalin in many of his books, such as *The Stalin School of Falsification*. Solzhenitsyn also dwelt on the theme of Stalin falsification in *The Gulag Archipelago* and other works, even accusing the present leaders of failing to tell the whole truth about the Stalin era and of perpetuating some of the late dictator's oppressions. But Solzhenitsyn had more luck than Trotsky: the United States, Britain, West Germany, Norway, and Switzerland offered him immediate asylum.

The "numbers game" concerning the quantity of political prisoners in the Soviet Union has become a kind of worldwide speculation. Estimates of the number of prison inmates range from 12 million in Stalin's day—about half of them "politicals"—to 2 million today, according to some sources. Peter Reddaway, a British specialist on the USSR, who lectures at the London School of Economics, claims that there are actually about 10,000 political prisoners now in the USSR.

Many Soviet officials are still darkly, and probably justifiably, suspicious of contact between dissidents and foreigners. Now and then they have warned foreign correspondents about meetings with certain activists. In addition, the party organs have attacked Soviet writers and artists for trying to smuggle their works abroad and, at the same time, have issued an implied threat that they faced official blacklisting—and hence loss of artistic livelihood at home—for their actions.

Foreigners have in fact been the conduits for smuggling thousands of manuscripts out of the Soviet Union, including the previous works by Solzhenitsyn. Just one Western organization, Radio Liberty, located in Munich and subsidized by America, admits having gathered a library of more than two thousand samizdat, or self-published documents, totaling over twelve thousand pages.[4] The "underground railroad" for taking these manuscripts to the West has been picturesquely described as a Byzantine operation full of CIA and KGB agents, hustling émigré organizations, and student couriers who are sometimes paid round-trip air fares of perhaps $1,200 between, say, Paris and Moscow, by enterprising publishers or middlemen.

Most critics of the USSR agree with the desire of dissident intellectuals who want to see the elimination of state censorship. While we call it censorship, the Soviets say that all Soviet literature must, in order to be published, conform to the standards of "socialist realism." In a word, socialist realism means that the truth about life is mainly ideological; reality, therefore, is to be seen not so much as it actually is but as it should be to correctly fulfill the goals of the community. Artists themselves do not determine what the goals are to be, or what changes are to be made; this is done by the party, which alone has the authority to say what is good or bad, even to the extent of rewriting yesterday's happenings.

To these ends, the party and the writers' unions in the USSR work hand in hand. The unions by their membership decide which writers are "in favor" or "out of favor." To be published, a writer often has to rewrite, delete, or add passages as suggested by officials of the writers' unions. If the writer refuses the suggestions, he can attempt to present his arguments to the officials, but only they will determine if his works are to appear legally in print. On the strength of their opinion, for example, Boris Pasternak's *Doctor Zhivago* was rejected for publication in the USSR. Indeed, it is said that through such administrative action no prose work of Pasternak was published in the Soviet Union since 1933.[5]

Harrison E. Salisbury, who edited *The Soviet Union: The Fifty Years,* says that in addition to censorship, the government and the party can bring pressure to bear on publishing houses that are run either directly by government agencies or by quasi-government agencies such as the writers' union or the Academy of Sciences. Often a word from the party's Central Committee may be enough to halt the publication of a book. On the other hand, says Salisbury, there is a small amount of leeway, of independence, or local flexibility. A manuscript rejected in Moscow may see the light of day in a Kazakh publication or one in Vladivostok. This may occur because a local man may be a good friend of the author.

How do literary personalities in the USSR explain the all-consuming censorship? Vsevolod Kochetov, a conservative Soviet novelist (he died in 1973) who wrote the popular propaganda novel *The Yershov Brothers* (it attacked disloyal writers), told Salisbury defensively that there were laws against pornography and publication of military secrets even in the United States. He suggested that some censorship over literature was desirable, an opinion that would have few defenders in the West. Another writer, Nicoláy Gribachev, told Salisbury that there was no censorship in the Soviet Union, only editorial tutelage.

Yevgény Yevtushenko, the lanky "poet of the pro-letariat," is usually regarded in the USSR as a loyal in-tellectual. Some Westerners have even dubbed him a "safe Establishment poet." But he sometimes surprises the Establishment with his independence. In the 1960s he wrote a few poems such as "Babi Yar" that irritated party leaders. "Babi Yar" was based on the Nazi mas-sacre of Jews in the Ukraine. (Not only Jews were killed by Nazis, say the Soviets.) After Solzhenitsyn's arrest, Yevtushenko, who once called Solzhenitsyn "our only living classic," rushed a telegram of protest to Soviet leader Leonid Brezhnev. "I was shaken by this news," he said later in a statement circulated in Moscow explaining his protest. He added that he was "extremely agitated over both the writer's personal fate and public repercussions over the arrest." Yevtushenko even defended Solzhenitsyn's book, *Gulag.* Although he did not, said Yevtushenko, agree with many of Sol-zhenitsyn's opinions, he was shocked to find so much ig-norance about the Stalinist oppression among present-day Soviet youth.[6]

For this dissident outburst Yevtushenko was called a "political infant" by Establishment writers and edi-tors. Indeed, editorial members of the weekly newspa-per of the writers' union, *Literaturnaya Gazeta,* com-plained that Yevtushenko was not only rash but also unable to "sort out the complexities of the present-day ideological struggle with the West." There was a veiled threat that the poet ought to heed his colleagues' ad-vice about orthodoxy.

But the Establishment's displeasure went beyond mere words. Yevtushenko's next poetry recital was abruptly canceled. At these recitals, Yevtushenko draws thousands of spectators.

Reprisals had already affected some well-known friends and supporters of Solzhenitsyn, for example, the famed cellist Mstislav Rostropovich, who in 1974 was given permission to live in the West. Solzhenitsyn had sometimes lived in the cellist's home. Now Rostropovich reported the cancellation of one or more of his concerts, including an overseas booking. A dissident in his own right, Rostropovich had once written a letter to *Pravda,* the party organ, and other Soviet papers, praising Solzhenitsyn's literary and intellectual talents and defending the right of every man to think independently and without fear. The Rostropovich letter mentioned that at one time there were official lists of "forbidden works" by such composers as Shostakóvich, Prokófiev, and Kachaturián.[7] *Pravda* never printed the letter.

Another dissident writer, Lidiya Chukovskaya, also had given public support to both Solzhenitsyn and dissident physicist Sakharov and had let Solzhenitsyn use her home outside Moscow. She was expelled from the writers' union in January 1974. Yevtushenko reported that one writer who had come to Miss Chukovskaya's defense learned that some of his own works scheduled for publication were now refused publication. Thus, defenders of Solzhenitsyn's defenders were under attack. Another writer, said Yevtushenko, who had gone to Solzhenitsyn's Moscow apartment after his arrest to show his support was himself under the threat of expulsion from the writers' union and anyone who defended him might be punished. Thus, Yevtushenko proved he was no "kept poet" of the Establishment, that on occasion he too wished to express dissent. Now, said Yevtushenko, he was worried about the fate of all Soviet writers. He perhaps need not have worried that much; the majority of writers' union members (virtually all the major Soviet writers except well-known dissidents) had no use for Solzhenitsyn's ideas or his literary works. Indeed, the writers' union had expelled the novelist as far back as 1969. Another Soviet novelist, Viktor P. Nekrasov, a chronicler of World War II, said in Moscow on March 11, 1974, that he was being pressured to join in denunciations of Solzhenitsyn and Sakharov in order to get his works published.

A few days after Solzhenitsyn was exiled to the West a poem appeared in the Soviet magazine *Yunost* (Youth), which some observers in Moscow believed was a veiled tribute to the novelist, although of course his name was not mentioned. Also, the poem could have symbolized all dissidents in the USSR. The poem, entitled "Not Completely," written by Borís Slutsky, spoke of a man who has been "humiliated, trampled upon, slandered [and] whispered against" but who nevertheless retains "like a gift bestowed by God, the answering blow."

Was it an allusion to the novelist? Or was it a kind of sermon for all the downtrodden and lonely? If it was the former, it indicated that Soviet censorship was not nearly as pervasive as one might believe.

Another poem appeared a few weeks later that left no doubt about its subject. It was entitled "Madame Solzh." Published in the Soviet humor magazine *Krokodil,* the poem minced no words, accusing Solzhenitsyn of prostituting his talent for foreign coin.[8]

2

SOLZHENITSYN: FROM MARXIST TO MYSTIC

Somebody who has learned to think can never be
deprived of freedom.

From the Soviet novel *Not by Bread Alone* by
Vladímir Dudintsev, 1956

Every artist of every country only harms himself by
remaining for long in a state of constant resentment,
for resentment devours his talent, and the writer
becomes so biased that the bias devours truth itself.

Yuri V. Bondarev,
Soviet writer and Lenin Prize winner
for literature,
1972 (commenting on *The Gulag Archipelago*)

Mr. Solzhenitsyn's banishment was unique in that he
had refused to bow to intense and unrelenting official pressures, refused to quit his homeland volun-
tarily, and had to be deported with an escort of eight
security agents.

Hedrick Smith,
New York Times, 1974

Aleksándr I. Solzhenitsyn not only bolted from Marxism but he embraced Christianity, and one of his first acts in exile was to kneel in prayer at a Swiss chapel. Many factors combined to loosen Solzhenitsyn's Marxist moorings during his youth. They included Stalin's personality cult and the sweeping purges of the 1930s which are said to have hurt the Red Army's ability to resist the Nazi invasion and thus added to the toll in blood and tears of the Russian people. As a soldier, Solzhenitsyn was personally aware of the unprecedented casualties among Soviet fighting men.

While he lived in the Soviet Union and clashed verbally with the Kremlin, Solzhenitsyn's utterances and even his physical appearance, with his Lincolnesque beard and doleful eyes, lent him a martyr's image. He had said: "Let the first bayonet come and pierce me." "Kill me quickly because I write the truth about Russian history." "I am ready to meet death at any moment." "I am bound hand and foot." "I am gagged." Solzhenitsyn symbolized the solitary figure arrayed against impossible odds.

It was this image plus his generally acclaimed literary talent that increased Solzhenitsyn's popularity and helped make his books as sought after as the proverbial forbidden fruit. Probably he could never have fit into Communist orthodoxy. In his book *The Cancer Ward,* Solzhenitsyn is obviously in full accord with the character who says he will never accept a "final word" on anything from the party.

Aleksándr Isayevich Solzhenitsyn was born in Kislovódsk, in the foothills of the northern Caucasus in 1918, one year after the October Revolution that overthrew Kerensky's government. His father was an office worker who died when Aleksándr was a boy. *Current Biography* says Solzhenitsyn is descended from Cossack intellectuals. Soviet critics, anxious to find causes for his dissent, have impugned Solzhenitsyn as the offspring of "alien" and "socially hostile" capitalists and landowners who were overthrown by the Bolshevik Revolution. The *Literaturnaya Gazeta,* after criticizing Solzhenitsyn, offered this mocking comment: "We were naturally far from looking for a direct, vulgar sociological connection between on the one hand a person's origin, his milieu during adolescence and his education, and on the other hand, his activity as an adult." But it is obvious the magazine wanted its readers to draw this parallel.[1]

Kostoglostov, a chief character in *The Cancer Ward,* whose ideas reflect the author's, gets into a heated argument about lineage. When someone declares that behind all greed and selfishness is always found a bourgeois origin, Kostoglostov is infuriated and retorts that this "social-origins" idea is not Marxism but racism. This remark is nothing but ideological subversion, he is told, whereupon he replies with a string of curses.

We get other glimpses of Solzhenitsyn's youthful disaffection in his book *First Circle.* For example, Gleb Nerzhin, a prisoner who is the author's counterpart, says he was only twelve years old when he opened a newspaper that told of some engineers who were accused of sabotage. Although he didn't know exactly why, young Gleb could not believe that engineers could be capable of wantonly destroying things. (But some Soviet engineers and technicians as well as high officials were not so pure-hearted. See, for example, an abbreviated eyewitness story of actual sabotage at high levels, written by John D. Littlepage, an American engineer who worked many years in the USSR, in *The Reader's Digest,* October, 1938).

Solzhenitsyn attended Rostóv University, where he studied mathematics and physics. An ambitious youth, he at the same time enrolled in a correspondence course in writing at an institute in Moscow. In 1941, the year Germany invaded the USSR, Solzhenitsyn graduated from Rostóv University. Almost immediately he was drafted into the Red Army and, because of his background, was sent to artillery school. Later he was appointed commander of an artillery battery, and saw a good deal of combat, winning several decorations.

Tragedy for Solzhenitsyn struck early in 1945. As a Red Army captain Solzhenitsyn took liberties, such as putting thinly disguised attacks about Marshal Stalin in letters to an army friend. He wrote that Stalin was an inept strategist and a poor linguist. Whatever the merits of this criticism, the war was still on and the mails were censored. He was arrested, his shoulder boards torn off, and he was sentenced to eight years in a labor camp. Later, Solzhenitsyn admitted his letter writing was a "childish piece of stupidity." [2]

Many Soviet citizens believe that the real reason for Solzhenitsyn's imprisonment was that he had declared it was senseless for the Red Army to take such heavy casualties fighting the Germans on German soil, and that he "agitated" against carrying the war outside Russian soil. Whatever the reason, I have heard ordinary Soviet people espouse this belief about his imprisonment.

Solzhenitsyn tells of an unforgettable incident that occurred as he was being led under arrest from the battlefield. Suddenly he heard his name called. He stopped. It was the brigade commander, and he reached out his hand to Solzhenitsyn and wished him good luck. It was a daring act for the commander. But if the incident helped to lighten Solzhenitsyn's misery it did nothing to shorten his term of punishment.

Solzhenitsyn's entry into prison was perhaps similar to the story of prisoner Innokenty Volodin in *First*

Circle, who is taken to the same prison Solzhenitsyn first saw in 1945: the old Lubyanka. Innokenty looks up before entering and observes a concealed searchlight on a turret above the building and two stone naiads gazing impudently at the citizens below. Once inside, he sees peepholes and locks and a sign that says: "Reception for arrested persons." He notices with horror how the stone steps have a deep concavity, having been worn down by the passage of countless thousands of prisoners and their guards over many years. Innokenty is forced to stand naked before the arresting officers. He is morally degraded. Shorn of all possessions, he is then left in a cubicle not much larger than a dog kennel. Few other authors have portrayed the act of arrest so vividly and terrifyingly.

In *Gulag* Solzhenitsyn tells us he himself had an impulse to yell when he was being transferred from the car to the Lubyanka. But he kept still. In retrospect he says that if he had shouted his innocence on the streets only two hundred people at most would have heard him. With the publication of *Gulag* he hoped to reach 200 million Russians. (He would certainly reach a large English-speaking audience, as almost three million copies of *Gulag* were scheduled for American publication, as reported in June, 1974.) But, thinking back, Solzhenitsyn believes he may have been cowardly in keeping silent; that perhaps he was merely trying to placate his guards.[3]

What impact does arrest have on one's psyche? Can the psychological marks left by such a shattering experience ever be erased? The French writer Albert Camus, reflecting on the effect of prison life on a man's character, wrote that many years in prison do not produce a very conciliatory form of intelligence. "If the mind is strong enough to construct in a prison cell a moral philosophy that is not one of submission, it will generally be one of domination." There is the likelihood that a man who has spent years in prison will come to hate the authorities who put him there. As everyone knows, while he remained inside the Soviet Union, Solzhenitsyn was a fierce and unrelenting critic.

Stalin died March 5, 1953. On that day Solzhenitsyn was released from his prison camp only to begin a three-year term of enforced exile in Soviet Central Asia. He taught school and in his spare time began to jot down some of the ideas and stories that he had kept in the recesses of his mind over many years. It is this experience as a teacher that serves as background for the author's short story "Matryona's House." Incidentally, while in a prison camp Solzhenitsyn developed a cancerous tumor and was treated, apparently successfully, at various clinics. Life in such a clinic is portrayed in his novel *The Cancer Ward,* one of the author's least controversial novels.

In 1956 Solzhenitsyn was released from exile and officially rehabilitated. A historic milestone occurred that year when party leader Nikíta Khrushchév, addressing the Twentieth Party Congress in Moscow, February 24–25, strongly denounced Stalin, giving many details about his barbaric rule. There was strong reaction against one-man rule and the cult of personality. The period of de-Stalinization, dating from this speech, helped launch Solzhenitsyn's literary career. Six years later, the novel *One Day in the Life of Ivan Denisovich* appeared in print. All copies of the book and the magazine in which it was also published were quickly gobbled up. The book gave an almost surgically penetrating look at one very bleak prison camp in Siberia.

One Day had special significance because it was one of the first works to be published in the Soviet Union that openly admitted what had been reported in the

West for a long time: the blight of countless prison camps in that country. There were a few other attempts to portray the prison experiences of the Stalin epoch, but Solzhenitsyn's book had the merit of true artistry. In *One Day* the reader feels as if he himself is undergoing the ordeal of camp life.

In the camp the inmates resemble caged animals scrounging for gruel, rotten fish, and cabbage leaves. A prisoner's most important possessions are a spoon, a needle and thread, his boots. Some critics called *One Day* the most startling book ever published in the Soviet Union. The late editor Aleksándr Tvardóvsky was so impressed when he first read the manuscript that although he was in bed he got up and put on a suit and tie before he continued reading.[4] The poet Samuel Marshak wrote flatteringly of *One Day* in *Pravda* (January 30, 1964). (But an editorial in that paper pointed out that the book was not outstanding enough to be worthy of the Lenin Prize.)[5] Outside of the USSR, *One Day* was so popular that it was published widely in the Eastern European countries and Cuba as well as in the West.

Soviet authorities candidly admitted the uniqueness and importance of the publication of *One Day*. Thus, Yekaterína Fúrtseva, the Soviet Minister of Culture, said in an interview in *Le Monde* in 1969 that "in issuing *One Day in the Life of Ivan Denisovich* the Soviet Union published a testimony, the like of which has never been written in any other country." But not everything was smooth sailing for Solzhenitsyn, and it is said that Nikíta Khrushchév himself had to exert influence to get the work published. Also lending his weight was Aleksándr Tvardóvsky, the then editor of the important literary magazine *Novy Mir,* who had become a close friend of the author's.

One Day, in fact, signaled Solzhenitsyn's future literary feud with the Soviet regime. Some leading Soviet writers criticized the book for its feeling of hopelessness. It was "morally limited," they said. This criticism was later to be leveled against most of the novelist's works, including *First Circle* and *The Cancer Ward*. Nikolay Gribachev, an editor quoted by Harrison E. Salisbury in his comprehensive book *The Soviet Union: The Fifty Years*, said that *One Day* was "very narrow" and that Ivan Denisovich lacked any nobility of character. But more sweeping criticism came from writer Galina Serebryakova, who said that Solzhenitsyn was very provincial in his approach and had just scratched the surface of the problem, thereby preventing a more profound study of the Stalinist prison life. (She herself had been arrested in the Stalinist purges.) Some critics in the West say that Solzhenitsyn succeeded in such an in-depth study of the labor camps in his work *The Gulag Archipelago*. Needless to say, the official Soviet opinion of *Gulag* was that it slandered the Soviet government and people. As noted, it was *Gulag*, smuggled to the West and published in various editions in December 1973, together with his political writings that especially irked the Kremlin and directly led to a confrontation and later the author's deportation.

For the Kremlin, *Gulag* is no doubt the most dangerous anti-Soviet book to come from Solzhenitsyn's pen. *Gulag* is anti-October Revolution. Solzhenitsyn says the regime betrayed the people, that its blunders and crimes killed great numbers of Red Army soldiers in World War II, that these blunders actually caused mass desertions to the Germans. In *Gulag* Solzhenitsyn dispenses with caution in his effort to indict the Soviet regime before the world. He even raises the question of what would have happened if the millions of Soviet citizens who were about to be arrested and sent to Siberian penal camps had, instead, put up armed resistance.

In this all-pervasive attack on the system, especially the Stalinist system, Solzhenitsyn cites cases from personal experience, from rumors plus the recollections of 200 others who knew about or themselves suffered under Stalin's yoke. Moreover, Solzhenitsyn said he had several sequels to *Gulag* that contained more salvos against the regime. The author said he had intended to delay publication of *Gulag* in order to protect his sources (many of whom are still alive) but that he decided to publish the book in the West after the KGB seized parts of the manuscript from a friend who reportedly committed suicide as a result.

Actually, the late Soviet Communist Party leader Nikíta Khrushchév preceded *Gulag* by more than fifteen years with an official exposé and condemnation of Stalinism, including many lurid details of Stalin's crimes. In *Gulag*, however, Solzhenitsyn stabs at the very foundations of the Soviet regime and raises the question of the culpability of the present Soviet leadership.

One Day was the first and last major work of Solzhenitsyn to be published with permission in the Soviet Union. Only a few of his short stories were later published with the approval of Glavlit, the official censorship body. After Khrushchév was removed from leadership in October 1964, Solzhenitsyn's literary productions met with increasing disapproval.

To get the popular short story "Matryona's House" published, Solzhenitsyn's friend Tvardóvsky helped override opposition. The story tells of a man (modeled after the author himself) who comes to a village in Soviet Central Asia to teach and boards at the home of an old woman who struggles uncomplainingly in order to live. She is finally killed in a horrible railroad accident. Matryona's house is filthy: there are cockroaches about and a lame cat. Nobody offers her any help or kindness even though she is constantly helping others. This, said Solzhenitsyn's critics, was a defamation of Soviet life. Where, they asked, does one find such a lonely person as Matryona in the USSR? Indeed, Matryona seems to be the Russian embodiment of kindness and self-sacrifice, and in a ringing finale the author declares that everybody who lived near her or knew her never understood that she was "that righteous one without whom, as the proverb says, no village can stand. . . . Nor any city. . . . Nor our whole land." Some Soviet specialists like American journalist Anthony Astrachan have even called this story the best in post-Stalin Russian literature.[6]

Most of Solzhenitsyn's other works have elicited harsh criticism and have not been published in the Soviet Union. One is the *Feast of the Conquerors,* a play that deals with reprisals against Soviet soldiers who are coming home after having been prisoners of war. It is considered an anti-Soviet work. (But Solzhenitsyn had often said he did not want this work to be read.) According to *Feast* the Red Army consists of a bunch of blockheads, marauders, and vandals, living only for their own pleasure. It is hardly a theme to recommend the author to his countrymen. The play was also considered to be sympathetic to the Vlasov troops. Andréi Vlasov was a Red Army general who defected to the Nazis in World War II and was later executed when the Western Allies handed him over to the Red Army. Understandably, the Soviets are not pleased to see favorable material written about a traitor.

A Solzhenitsyn work, called simply *A Play by Aleksándr Solzhenitsyn,* was staged in 1970 in Minneapolis. Again, there is the prison motif. One of the inmates describes the prison as "the invisible nation, the country that's not in the history books, the geography books, the psychology books." The camp is of course a symbol of Stalin's totalitarian state. Most of the prisoners are there for political reasons, for example, failing to inform on a friend. Fear, boredom, corruption, lies are all part of camp life, which is a living hell.

But not all Soviet prison life is hellish. In *First Circle*, Gleb Nerzhin is one of those privileged prisoners assigned to a sharashka. The prison-run scientific institute to which he is assigned is working on electronic eavesdropping devices; one of its tasks is to listen in to tapes of telephone calls by Russians and foreigners in Moscow. The sharashka is a society within a society. In it, life is immeasurably better than in an ordinary prison camp. Meat is available and books. Even love is possible.

When Gleb Nerzhin (who obviously speaks for Solzhenitsyn) is asked to lend his talent to develop a special device to catch unsuspecting persons, he refuses, thereby condemning himself to be transferred back to a regular prison and its terrible indignities. It is Nerzhin's way of protest. In contrast to him is Lev Rubin, described as a brainwashed Communist, who has convinced himself it is all right to work on a "voice-printer" that eventually helps trap the diplomat Innokenty, sending him to the Lubyanka.

There is bitter irony in Nerzhin's remark that only those people in prison are truly free to be honest with each other. ("When you've robbed a man of everything, he's no longer in your power—he's free again.") The book ends with another bit of irony: prisoners are being transported through Moscow on a meat van; that is, it is made to look like a meat van from the outside because the word *meat* is painted on the truck in different languages. A foreign journalist, seeing the van, writes a story about meat being plentiful in the capital.

Not only publication of his literary works in the West, or in samizdat inside the Soviet Union, but also his refusal to keep silent when he felt he ought to speak out landed Solzhenitsyn in constant hot water with the Establishment. Once, in May 1967, Solzhenitsyn wrote a characteristically critical letter to a meeting of Soviet writers in which he appealed for the lifting of censorship. He referred to Soviet writers who had been silenced in the 1920s, including Borís Pilnyák, Andréi Platónov, and Ósip Mandelshtám. He cited others who were "exposed to violence and personal persecution," such as Mikhaíl Bulgákov, Ánna Akhmátova, Borís Pasternak, Mikhaíl Zóshchenko, Aleksándr Grin, and Vasíly Gróssman. He said the public readings of his works had been canceled nine out of eleven times, that the manuscript of *First Circle* had been taken from him by security police in 1965, that *The Cancer Ward* was rejected by all the major literary journals in the USSR, that his short stories remained unavailable to the general public as they had never been printed in book form, and that his literary archives covering fifteen or twenty years had been confiscated. Solzhenitsyn concluded: "My work has thus been finally smothered, gagged, and slandered." [7]

Soviet reaction to Solzhenitsyn's works—with few exceptions—has been entirely negative. For example, Soviet critics have called *First Circle* provocative and a boon to Western propaganda. (Konstantín Fédin, a frequent literary spokesman for the Soviet Establishment, asked Solzhenitsyn in 1967 why he didn't speak out in protest against the "dirty use of your name by our enemies in the West.") [8] A representative Soviet view of *The Cancer Ward* was very punishing: "It makes you throw up when you read it." Solzhenitsyn has been called "an apologist for czarism" and (after publication of *Gulag*) likened to Herostratus, a fourth-century Greek who burned down the magnificent temple of Diana of Ephesus in an attempt to achieve fame. According to Western observers, the majority of Soviet public opinion appears not to favor Solzhenitsyn. Indeed, *Washington Post* correspondent in Moscow Robert G. Kaiser reported in January 1974 that many ordinary Soviet citizens had wanted both Solzhenitsyn and dissident physicist Andréi Sakharov punished.[9]

Aside from his books Solzhenitsyn's most heretical anti-Soviet declaration was contained in a fifteen thousand-word letter he sent to the Kremlin in September 1973 (and released to the West early in 1974). In the letter the novelist asked the Soviet authorities to think about abandoning communism and splitting off from the country its non-Russian republics. Marxism and industrialization, said Solzhenitsyn, were alien to Russian thinking. Suddenly, Western liberals and intellectuals who had hitherto saluted Solzhenitsyn's every act and statement, now wagged their heads. They saw him as one who wishes to jettison the machinery of the present for the ways of the past. In short, a reactionary. In the letter, Solzhenitsyn also displayed anti-Western and antidemocratic thinking. Curiously, the letter was altered; that is, the text that was mailed to the Kremlin and that which was released in the West six months later were different. In the Western version, Solzhenitsyn had deleted or toned down some of his negative opinions of Western democracy. The novelist claimed he was being misrepresented by the press. But the fact is that the text reaching the West had been changed, perhaps so as not to grate on Western and especially American sensibilities.[10]

In mid-April 1974 dissident scientist Andréi Sakharov circulated a 4,000-word reply to Solzhenitsyn's 15,000-word open letter to the Kremlin. The open letter and Sakharov's rejoinder resembled a public debate of sorts between two prominent dissidents.

Sakharov concurred in some of Solzhenitsyn's ideas but the disagreements between the two men outweighed their agreements. Sakharov criticized the "nationalist and isolationist direction" of the author's thinking. He scored Solzhenitsyn's emphasis on Great Russian nationalism and his rejection of global cooperation, saying this was not only wrong but "potentially dangerous." Solzhenitsyn had, for example, advocated the development of Siberia; but Sakharov advised that Siberian development could not advance smoothly without big imports of foreign capital and technology. (This segment of the debate had an element of sterility as in mid-1974 foreign businessmen, mostly Japanese, were reported nearing agreement with the Soviet Union on collaborative development of energy sources in Siberia.) In addition, Sakharov took issue with Solzhenitsyn's stress on the "threat from China" and he said that the writer had exaggerated the role of ideology in the Soviet Union. According to Sakharov, ideology was more a facade used by the Kremlin to maintain the system than anything else.

Like Solzhenitsyn, Sakharov asked the regime to renounce Marxism but he assailed the author for his rejection of Marxism as an "alien" import from the West. Ideas, said the scientist, should be judged solely on their merits, not their origin. Sakharov and Solzhenitsyn were also at opposite poles on the subject of religion, with Solzhenitsyn desiring to replace Marxism with a revival of church authority, that is, the Russian Orthodox Church. This idea, said Sakharov, was "utopian and fraught with danger." He also challenged the author's contention that the Soviet Union was not yet ripe for democracy.

Nevertheless, Sakharov paid his respects to Solzhenitsyn's talent. He said he bowed in praise before *Gulag* and he described this work as "accurate," "uncompromising" and ". . . (full of) deep illumination." He saw Solzhenitsyn as a "giant in the struggle for human dignity." The nuclear physicist also agreed with the author's proposal for ending Soviet hegemony in Eastern Europe and in the non-Russian republics of the USSR.

Commenting on the Sakharov-Solzhenitsyn variance, some observers saw a parallel in Russian history between Slavophiles and admirers of Western culture. Broadly speaking, Solzhenitsyn was the Slavophile and Sakharov the internationalist. The British Broadcasting Corporation called the Sakharov-Solzhenitsyn rift "one of the major debates of the century." But the Soviet Establishment saw it as an irrelevancy; the *Literaturnaya Gazeta* said it added nothing to the atmosphere but "delirium."

Here are more of Solzhenitsyn's views gleaned from his books:

On exile: In *First Circle* the author has a character say that exile is "spiritual castration." (Before joining her husband in exile in late March 1974, Mrs. Solzhenitsyn, who may be said to mirror her husband's opinions, told Western journalists that "no one had the power to separate Solzhenitsyn's spiritual link with Russia.") [11]

On the value of a great writer: "For a country to have a great writer is like having a second government." (*First Circle.*)

Was Solzhenitsyn thinking of himself when he wrote this? Probably. Despite his unquestioned courage and perseverance, humility is not part of the Solzhenitsyn temperament. He himself tells us that while he was still in a labor camp he began to rehearse the speech for his anticipated Nobel Prize for literature.[12] (He won the prize in 1970.) As a schoolboy the novelist exhibited cockiness. A childhood friend (who was later arrested with Solzhenitsyn on the battlefield; then the friendship turned into enmity) tells us that Solzhenitsyn used to put into his personal notebooks such titles as "Complete Works, Vol. I, Part I."

On mendacity: "If no one is allowed for decade after decade to tell it as it is, the mind becomes irreparably deluded, and finally it becomes harder to comprehend one's own compatriot than a man from Mars." (*The Cancer Ward.*)

On linguistics: Solzhenitsyn is a purist who believes the Russian language should not be corrupted with any foreign words or new words, but should, instead, use good old-fashioned Russian words. A character in *First Circle* echoes Solzhenitsyn's own desire to purify the language, saying that the word for *capitalism* (pronounced almost the same in Russian as in English) should be replaced with an old Russian word that is the literary equivalent of moneybagism. Solzhenitsyn also attacked Stalin, who was far from being a purist, on linguistics. Stalin once said that language serves as a means of communication of a people—not one class to the prejudice of other classes. Such a language would not be changed by revolutions and could serve different social systems equally well. This view was contained in a letter Stalin wrote to *Pravda* that appeared in the June 20, 1950 issue. In *Gulag* Solzhenitsyn condemns the Soviet regime for denying a people (the Yenisei Ostyaks) a newly developed alphabet and vocabulary, leaving this people without any written language, except presumably the Russian.

Of course, in the USSR or any modern nation a single language is a powerful unifying force, especially in a country with great diversity of nationality with evidence now and then of local chauvinism. But according to Solzhenitsyn's long letter to the Kremlin, made available to the West in March 1974, the author preferred to see the Soviet Union split up.

After his involuntary exile, Soviet authorities predicted oblivion for the world-famed author. But at least for the forseeable future Solzhenitsyn was assured of international public attention. Even the huge American labor union, A.F.L.-C.I.O., invited him in March 1974 to tour the United States under its sponsorship. (Solzhenitsyn declined "with great gratitude.") Meanwhile, many Western writers and intellectuals regarded Solzhenitsyn as an authentic hero and martyr and continued to write about him dithrambically.

3

SAKHAROV:
CIVIL RIGHTS CHAMPION

Intellectual freedom is essential to human society—
freedom to obtain and distribute information, freedom for open-mindedness and unfearing debate
and freedom from pressure by officialdom
and prejudices.

Andréi D. Sakharov,
from "Thoughts about Progress, Peaceful Coexistence and Intellectual Freedom," 1968

The problem is not whether Sakharov enjoys intellectual freedom—there are no doubts about that—
but how and with what purposes he uses it.

Mstislav V. Kéldysh,
president of the Soviet Academy of Sciences,
October 1973

"I developed a moral consciousness gradually in the 1950s; I suppose the turning point came when I sent a letter of protest to the government against our atomic tests in 1958—and then again in 1961." That is how nuclear physicist Andréi D. Sakharov described, in an interview in his Moscow apartment, his journey from loyal scientist to dissenting intellectual. Sakharov began to speak out, preaching against the arbitrary use of state power and in favor of more freedom and flexibility in education and other fields. In his 1961 protest letter he urged Soviet leader Nikíta Khrushchév not to go ahead with testing a one-hundred-megaton nuclear warhead in the atmosphere because of possible risks to health. The reply he got was that he shouldn't meddle in politics, that on the world stage the Soviet Union absolutely required a position of strength.[1] Indeed, Sakharov says the regime actually tried to find "compromising material" on him in order to "teach him a lesson." But apparently he had a very clean record.

Later, Sakharov began attending the court trials of so-called freethinkers—as dissidents are often called. Often he couldn't get inside the courtroom: it was either packed solid with security agents and no seats were available, or else authorities viewed him as a "troublemaker" and denied him entry. Sometimes on wintry days in bitter cold, Andréi Sakharov could be found outside a courtroom keeping vigil while a dissident—perhaps a friend—was on trial within. Thus, Sakharov the nuclear scientist gained a reputation as champion of oppressed intellectuals. Outside the USSR he became known for his writings and activities concerning human rights. In the early 1970s he himself was being harassed by authorities, and this engendered support for him in the West. Many American and European scientists and scholars, as well as the mass media, took up the cudgels in his behalf. At least one university, Princeton, offered him a teaching job. (Late in 1973 Sakharov announced for the first time that he had applied to Soviet authorities for permission to teach at Princeton, saying he would return to Moscow after a year or so.) [2]

The Kremlin may have been goaded into self-reflection, to wonder why some of the nation's best scientific (and literary) brains were joining the dissident ranks. Had something gone awry with Marxist-Leninist teaching? Could it be—the authorities may have questioned themselves—that the dissidents had even a slight "justification" for protest? Such soul-searching may actually have occurred, because in March 1974 *Pravda* published on its front pages a strong call for creation of a New Soviet Man. The paper said that all citizens should strive to make themselves morally perfect in their private as well as public lives. Of course the phrase "all citizens" could refer even to those at the pinnacle of power.

Doctor Sakharov's defection from orthodoxy was especially lugubrious in the eyes of officialdom. When a writer is infected by non-Marxist thinking it is one thing, but when a man of Sakharov's knowledge and stature goes the same route it is a more serious matter. Sakharov was one of the elite; he was a worker on top-secret projects and was widely regarded as the "father of the Soviet hydrogen bomb." He was a member of the prestigious Soviet Academy of Sciences. For his scientific achievements he had received numerous awards, including the Order of Lenin and a Stalin Prize. Soviet expert Harrison E. Salisbury once called him "Oppenheimer, Teller, and Hans Bethe all rolled into one." [3]

Andréi Dmitrievich Sakharov, the son of a physicist, was born May 21, 1921. He is sometimes described as a "Soviet physicist and social philosopher." Indeed, for over a dozen years the problems of international politics, as well as those of his own society, have occupied his thoughts. He graduated from Moscow University in 1942 with a degree in physics. The war was on, but such was the excellence of his work that he was exempt from military service and allowed to pursue scientific research throughout the war. In 1945 he joined the famous Lébedev Physics Institute of the Soviet Academy of Sciences in Moscow. Two years later he obtained his doctorate under the tutelage of Ígor Tamm, a savant and Nobel Prize winner in physics. Sakharov was but twenty-six years old, which was a young age to receive this advanced degree.

Between 1948 and 1956 Sakharov lived in a world sealed off from normal society. Engaged in nuclear weapons research, he had a twenty-four-hour bodyguard. (Once he was able, as a joke, to shake off his bodyguard and go skiing alone.) [4] In 1953 Sakharov became one of the youngest men ever to be elected to full membership in the Soviet Academy of Sciences.

He met his wife, Yelena, in 1970 during a lengthy vigil outside a courtroom where Sakharov went to advocate an open trial system. He failed. Yelena, a pediatrician, is half-Armenian and half-Jewish. Her mother was once exiled to Siberia during the Stalin purge trials. Yelena is a friendly and vivacious woman with a cigarette frequently held between her fingers. She is the aunt of Eduard Kuznetsov, a young Soviet Jew who was given a death sentence—later reduced to fifteen years—for the attempted hijack of a Soviet plane in 1970.

Before his plunge into unorthodoxy he drew a salary the equivalent of $26,500 a year.[5] He has since managed to live satisfactorily on a reduced income, which he has voluntarily made public: 400 rubles a month as an academician plus another 350 rubles as a resident worker at the institute. His total is 750 rubles, or about $800. Sakharov disclosed that he once had savings of $150,000 but had donated this amount to a hospital.

The nuclear physicist startled the world in 1968 when he issued his famous ten-thousand-word manifesto entitled "Thoughts on Progress, Coexistence, and Intellectual Freedom," which was circulated clandestinely in the USSR in samizdat and published in the West. The manifesto, although somewhat dated, is still worthy of study because of its precise reasoning and compelling logic; and at least some of its ideas still retain their original freshness. It urged not only a rapprochement with the West but also called for an ultimate convergence of communism and capitalism. For this purpose Sakharov offered a blueprint for Soviet-American cooperation by the year 2000.

The introduction contains these ringing words:

> The division of mankind threatens it with destruction. Civilization is imperiled by: a universal thermonuclear war, catastrophic hunger for most of mankind, stupefaction from the narcotic of "mass culture" and bureaucratized dogmatism, a spreading of mass myths that puts entire peoples and continents under the power of cruel and treacherous demagogues, and destruction or degeneration from the unforeseeable consequences of swift changes in the conditions of life on our planet.

Sakharov offers an antidote:

> In the face of these perils, any action increasing the division of mankind, any preaching of the incompatibility of world ideologies and nations, is madness and a crime. Only universal cooperation under conditions of intellectual freedom and the lofty moral ideals of socialism and labor, accompanied by the elimination of dogmatism and pressures of the concealed interests of the ruling classes, will preserve civilization . . .

But Sakharov was critical also of Soviet restrictions on writers and other intellectuals, and he attacked continuing censorship as a threat to intellectual freedom.

The physicist said that this freedom was "essential to human society—freedom to obtain and distribute information, freedom for open-minded and unfearing debate and freedom from pressure by officialdom and prejudices." The breadth of Sakharov's design is shown in the next sentence: "Such a trinity of freedom of thought is the only guarantee against an infection of people by mass myths which in the hands of treacherous hypocrites and demogogues can be transformed into bloody dictatorship." This was an obvious reference to the Stalinist terror.

Sakharov then took the Soviet regime to task for the arrest and detention of dissidents. He said that censorship of Soviet artists and of political literature had already compromised the Communist system. He also echoed his friend Aleksándr Solzhenitsyn, saying that "the exposure of Stalinism still had a long way to go." (In 1974 he still believed this for he said in a statement that the Soviet people were "still living in the spiritual atmosphere created by that era.") [6]

In 1970 Sakharov added to his credentials as a dissident when he helped establish the nongovernmental Committee on Human Rights. Its members included Solzhenitsyn and other writers, scholars, and intellectuals.

Then, in 1973, Sakharov collided head-on with his government when he took the extreme position of asking the United States to require the democratization of the USSR as a condition for détente with the Soviets. Sakharov later softened his position, saying he was not at all an opponent of détente, trade, or disarmament, but was merely opposed to what he called a "false détente" or a "capitulation détente." But his August 1973 statement that Soviet-American rapprochement would be very dangerous for both the USSR and the world was quite plain. I was one of the foreign reporters seated in Sakharov's apartment when he made the statement in which he used the word "danger" at least four times in referring to the implications of détente or rapprochement.

Here is the English translation of one pertinent passage that he read in Russian to those assembled:

> Rapprochement with the West would be very dangerous in that it would not solve any of the world's problems and would mean simply capitulation in terms of our real or exaggerated strength; that would mean an attempt at trade, to get from us gas and oil, neglecting all other aspects of the problem. I think it's very dangerous, dangerous because it might lead to very hard consequences inside our country and contaminate a whole world with antidemocratic traits. . . . I think that rapprochement without any qualification, accepting our own rules, will have a very bad consequence for our country and for the future of the world as a whole.

For taking such a position, virtually akin to political apostasy, Sakharov was sharply criticized. He was called a "traitor to the motherland," his meetings with foreign correspondents were lampooned, he and his wife were interrogated by the KGB, and many of his colleagues joined in attacking his statement. In one barrage, forty fellow academicians rebuked him. Later, dozens of prominent writers spoke out against Sakharov and other "freethinkers." Mstislav V. Kéldysh, president of the Soviet Academy of Sciences, called Sakharov a blind man politically and said that "Sakharov causes harm to the interests not only of the Soviet Union but also the people of other countries that sincerely strive for relaxation of tensions and for international cooperation." [7] Kéldysh was replying to a letter from the American Academy of Sciences, which feared that Sakharov would suffer punishment for his outspokenness.

Pyotr Kápitsa, one of the best-known physicists in the Soviet Union, remained silent. Some Western observers said the Kremlin had put intense pressure on

Kápitsa, regarded as an independent thinker—Stalin had once placed him under house arrest—and on other intellectuals, thus making them hold their tongues. This is highly possible, although it could be that Kápitsa, like Roy Medvédev, the dissident historian and author of a comprehensive book on the Stalin era, *Let History Judge,* could not agree entirely with Sakharov's views.[8] Medvédev, in a statement of his own, implied that Sakharov had blundered when he had—like some American congressmen—said that U.S. trade concessions should be contingent upon Soviet allowance of free emigration. Such a step, said Medvédev, was "tactically wrong."

Only a handful of the regular dissenters came to Sakharov's defense. (Some newspapers in the West, such as the *New York Times,* said this silence epitomized the ruthlessness of the Soviet drive to suppress dissent.) But a few intellectuals, including Aleksándr Solzhenitsyn and novelist Vladímir Maksimov, not only applauded Sakharov but also suggested that he would make an excellent candidate for the Nobel Peace Prize.[9]

Sakharov has publicly supported freedom of Jewish emigration to Israel. But he has done more. For example, to protest the murder of Israeli athletes at the Munich Olympic Games in 1972, he and his stepchildren joined others in a small demonstration in front of the Lebanese Embassy in Moscow.[10] For this, Sakharov was detained briefly by the police. Then, in October 1973, two Arabs, claiming membership in the Black September guerrilla organization, came to his apartment and, according to Sakharov, threatened his life if he issued another pro-Israel statement. One of the callers said he had graduated from Patrice Lumumba University in Moscow. When Sakharov's wife, Yelena, asked them, "Do you want to kill us?" one of the men is said to have replied: "We can do worse things than kill you. We are ready to die for the sake of our country. We do not stop at anything." [11]

It seemed there was a kind of inevitability that brought together dissidents like Sakharov with Jewish intellectuals who wished to emigrate to Israel. Of course all dissenters desired more freedom of one sort or another. Some Jewish intellectuals sought freedom to emigrate, while others, more in the mainstream of Soviet dissidence, wanted expansion of intellectual freedom but had no interest in leaving the Soviet Union. All dissidents, moreover, had a common frailty: they were, as it were, all hanging on to the same floating log. Probably the Jews were a bit stronger internationally than many others because of their ability to stir up foreign opinion for their cause. It served the different dissident groups better if they could join forces, but disunity rather than unity was the rule. Sakharov, however, sympathized with nearly all dissident groups who wanted freedom of speech, freedom to write, and freedom to travel.

Solzhenitsyn, hearing about the Arab visit to the Sakharov home, was indignant. He dashed off a short letter to Sakharov in which he said that such potential acts of terrorism in the Soviet Union could not take place without the approval of Soviet security men. And the novelist vowed that if any bodily harm came to Sakharov, the real culprit would be the Soviet regime. He ended his letter in these words: "If they ever strike such a blow against you while I remain alive, I assure you that I shall dedicate what remains of my pen and my life so that the murderers will not triumph but will lose." [12]

Dr. Sakharov issued a statement of his beliefs in mid-April 1974—a four-thousand-word commentary on Solzhenitsyn's long (fifteen-thousand-word) open letter to the Kremlin. In it Sakharov renewed his support for a convergence of capitalism and communism. As significant fields for cooperation he cited the development of nuclear and thermonuclear energy, new food-raising technology, production of synthetic protein substitutes, urban problems, exploration of space, combating cancer and heart disease, and developing industrial technology not harmful to the environment. (Such cooperation in space exploration already is underway.) These tasks required multibillions in investments and joint efforts on a global scale.

I visited Sakharov at his apartment in August 1973. To get there I accepted a ride with another foreigner, a resident correspondent in Moscow, who parked his car two blocks from our destination "so as not to attract attention," as he put it. As it was raining hard we trotted to the tall, unostentatious building of black-red brick. I had wondered if there would be any security men watching the building, inside or outside, but I could not see anybody. We bounded up six or seven flights of stairs, as the elevator was "lost" someplace, and were ushered into a four-room apartment by Mrs. Sakharov. Seated around the physicist were seven or eight foreign journalists. The scene could have been anyplace in America or Europe where a professor was holding a seminar at his home, except that here nearly everybody had tape recorders in addition to pencils and pads.

Sakharov was speaking slowly and softly in Russian. A man at his right side was giving a running translation. Sometimes the correspondents who knew Russian made a correction in the translation. Sakharov is kindly, unpretentious, and very attentive to others. His hair is thinning. His eyes are alert and friendly. The immediate impression one gets is that he does not fit the description he is often given—"father of the Soviet hydrogen bomb." He looks more like a professor of philosophy than one who has helped manufacture weapons of mass destruction. After meeting and speaking with him, one can imagine that Sakharov feels remorse about his work on the bomb. But he denies having such sentiment. As Sakharov spoke, his wife, Yelena, looking trim in well-pressed white slacks, sat listening nearby, her chin cupped in her hands.

The physicist–social critic read a statement on détente and other pertinent matters and then he took questions on many subjects from the assembled reporters. I was particularly interested in Sakharov's relations with his colleagues and also the general issue of disaffection of Soviet scientists. I asked Sakharov: "Have any of your colleagues attempted to question your motives or to put pressure on you to change your views?" Sakharov replied: "No. Nobody tries to do it, with very few exceptions. They are isolated cases." Then I asked whether he interpreted such silence as indicating approval.

Sakharov: "More as a reluctance to take sides. [But] there are both cases."

Later the topic of his relations with Princeton University and the issue of freedom of emigration came up. I asked Sakharov: "What would happen if 10 percent of Soviet scientists decided they wanted to emigrate?"

Sakharov: "In the first place I am sure that 10 percent will never have this idea. So it is not realistic to put it that way. But if a greater number of scientists than at present wished to emigrate, that would be natural. Many scientists leave all countries, throughout the world; the problem of 'brain drain' is widely discussed but at the end, finally, it doesn't lead to any catastrophic results, or consequences. Science is international. Technological knowledge is also becoming international. And the place of residence of a scientist is now the personal affair of each one."

Academician Sakharov also spoke of his human rights activities and the so-called democratic movement. He said you could hardly call it a movement, that it was mainly certain people who had become victims of injustice, or who sympathized with them, and went to protest unjust trials and to voice concern for the health of the people involved. "It's not a movement. It's normal human activity," he said. "It doesn't have the character of political action."

He said it was impossible to predict what might happen to him, but added: "I would like to believe that the perfectly loyal character of my activities would be understood [by the authorities]."

4

JEWS IN THE USSR

What has been persecuted throughout half a century
of the Soviet system, persecuted almost unto death,
is the Jewish heritage: the religious practices and the
culture through which Jews come together to ac-
knowledge a common bond . . . Soviet Jewry
has all but ceased to exist as a unity. . . .

Peter Grose,
"The Kremlin and the Jews" (from *The Soviet
Union: The Fifty Years,* edited by
Harrison E. Salisbury)

There is no anti-Semitism in the Soviet Union, and
Judaism is not persecuted. Jews actively participate
in all spheres of the country's social, political, economic and cultural life. Soviet Jews are the equal of
their fellow-workers in plants and factories, on state
and collective farms, in scientific and cultural institu-
tions, newspaper and magazine editorial offices, etc.
Many outstanding scientists, writers, artists,
composers, etc., are Jews.

Alekséi Puzin,
"Religion in the USSR," Moscow

There has never been and there is no
anti-Semitism in the Soviet Union.

Alekséi Kosýgin,
statement in New York, 1967

Jewish groups and their friends in the West often declare that the decline and gradual demise of Jewish life and culture in the USSR (and the world) is the biggest tragedy facing contemporary Jews. On the other hand, the Kremlin claims that only in the Soviet Union—and nowhere in the West—has the so-called "Jewish problem" been solved and in a manner that pleases a majority of its Jewish citizens.

The Soviet Union has one of the world's largest Jewish populations, with about 3 million Jews. Some of them wish to emigrate to Israel, where they can immerse themselves in their own culture. Then there are the completely assimilated Jews who are not involved with religion or Jewish traditions. Many assimilated Soviet Jews say that the desire of other Jews to emigrate to Israel is incomprehensible to them; but they believe they should have the right to do so.

For years the Jewish state has looked upon the Soviet Union as a reservoir of new citizens. Israel has done nearly everything it can to encourage Jews in the advanced countries, especially the Soviet Union, to settle in Israel to build up that country's industrial and military strength. Israel has sought to stimulate worldwide Jewish identification with Israel and to persuade Jews wherever they may be to consider settling in their "spiritual home." At times the unreserved sympathy of Soviet Jews for Israel has both alarmed and enraged the Kremlin. For example, Moscow's Jews exulted when Israel's first diplomatic envoy, Mrs. Golda Meir, arrived in the USSR.[1] This demonstration of pro-Israel support came in the midst of the Cold War when the Soviet regime wished to "sanitize" the people from all foreign influences. The Kremlin found intolerable any display of chauvinism or religious fervor by Jewish intellectuals; and hundreds were placed in penal camps or executed.

Jewish emigration is a serious problem for the Soviet Union. But some experts say the problem has been exaggerated. Thus, Professor Dan Miron of Tel Aviv University, on a visit to Moscow in the summer of 1971 as head of an Israeli delegation of intellectuals, told an interviewer: "My general feeling is that, as a Jewish problem, the problem of emigration is overemphasized." [2] Of course, Miron said, for some Jews emigration was a "burning problem," and he hoped those who wanted to leave would be allowed to. "But," he added, "the majority of Jews in the Soviet Union are integrated and they will remain so." What many of these Jews wanted was contact with Jews in other countries. They did not wish to leave their Soviet homeland, said Miron.

Not everybody agrees with Professor Miron. And many of those who do not agree have insisted that the Soviet Union permit absolutely free emigration of its citizens. An example is Dr. Veniamin G. Levich, a Soviet scientist and academician who lost his job as head of a department at Moscow University after he applied for a passport to emigrate together with his family (his two sons are also scientists) to Israel. Scholars such as Levich speak of the "slow execution" of people like himself who have been denied permission to emigrate.[3] The reason Soviet authorities give for such refusal is that many scientists have worked on projects dealing with state security. But it is obvious the Soviets don't want to risk a chain reaction of defections, since many professional people including scientists are Jews.

In the early 1970s the Kremlin reluctantly began to grant permission for increased Jewish emigration to Israel. Some reports said the Soviet response was due to agitation by militant Jews inside the USSR plus foreign pressure. Whatever the reason, the Soviet government allowed about fifteen thousand Jews to leave for Israel in 1971, thirty thousand in 1972, and approximately thirty-four thousand in 1973.[4] (Official Soviet figures are higher.) Meanwhile, there were complaints of long delays in obtaining exit visas, of persons being hastily dismissed from their jobs and being harassed from the moment they applied for their exit permits. In 1972 the authorities had imposed an emigration tax ranging as high as $30,000 on educated Jews seeking to emigrate, on the grounds that the state had gone to considerable expense to educate these citizens and if they chose to forsake their homeland they had an obligation to repay the state. However, the Soviets suspended the tax early in 1973, apparently due in part to their desire for détente plus a tumult of foreign protest.

Probably the Soviet Union will never satisfy Western and Israeli demands on emigration or freedom of travel for Jews. For instance, despite the increase of Soviet Jewish emigration in recent years—above thirty thousand a year at times—some supporters of Israel in the United States Congress in 1974 were mentioning an emigration level as high as one hundred thousand a year.[5]

These members of Congress frankly admitted they wanted nothing less than to alter the domestic structure of the USSR, using trade, credits, and technological aid as clubs to exact internal reform. Some experts on Soviet affairs, however, warned that coercion could have a boomerang effect, causing more rather than fewer domestic controls. On the other hand, activist Jews in the USSR and their supporters in the West naturally clamored for increased pressure on the Kremlin and for more publicity about the plight of the Soviet Jews.

The rationale for applying pressure on the Kremlin was that if repression in the USSR and the right to free emigration were ignored in America, this would amount to acquiescence in Soviet tyranny. Thus, Senators Henry M. Jackson and Abraham Ribicoff and like-minded legislators have demanded liberalization of Soviet society as a precondition for increasing trade and other exchanges. This position was taken by physicist Andréi Sakharov in his controversial statement of August 1973. It has also been supported by such Jewish activists as Dr. Veniamin Levich, who has called for the elimination of frontiers when it comes to human rights.

But travel outside the borders of a communist country is not a right but a privilege. It is granted only to a relatively small number of well-deserving citizens. Moreover, the Kremlin claims that but for the intense propaganda generated by anti-Soviet organizations about the so-called Jewish problem in the USSR the number of emigration applications by Jews would be close to zero. The Soviets also feel that allowing Jews to emigrate to Israel provides soldiery to Israel for use against Arab nations friendly to Moscow; and that such emigrants were being used by Israel to populate the occupied territories. The Kremlin has insisted that Israel abandon all Arab lands taken in the June 1967 war and afterward in order to improve Soviet-Israeli relations.

In all the literature on this and related topics, some questions of future importance have hardly been plumbed. What, for example, would be the long-term effect on Soviet Jewry if the Soviets were to permit free emigration of Jews to Israel, prompted at least in part by intense efforts from abroad to stimulate religious or nationalistic zeal among Soviet Jews? What of the delicate question of "loyalty" or "reliability" of Jewish citizens? Will Jews be considered "internal emigrés" in the Soviet Union? In Aleksándr Solzhenitsyn's book, *First*

Circle, it is stated that during the October Revolution of 1917 and long afterward the word "Jew" had a connotation of greater reliability to the new regime than the word "Russian." It is not hard, though, to imagine that circumstances could be reversed so that the reliability of Jews in the Soviet Union could be seriously undermined with the government. Already there are reports of discrimination against Jews in high positions in the USSR; and the allegiance of officers of the Jewish faith in the Soviet Army may even now be officially suspect. There is the following case of dissent among former high-ranking military officers: In December 1973 three Jewish ex-colonels in the Soviet Army were actively seeking to emigrate to Israel. Two of them said they had formally renounced their Soviet citizenship and all three reported they were subjected to "continuing reprisals." One of the Jewish ex-colonels had won thirteen decorations including the coveted Order of the Red Banner. Because he was having no success in his desire to emigrate, he reportedly handed back his medals in March 1974.

Soviet officials, however, take pains to point out that most Soviet Jews are content to remain in their country as loyal citizens, and the officials even note that a few Soviet Jews who emigrated to Israel have chosen to return to the USSR.

The complexity of the problem is illustrated by an editorial, entitled "End of a Culture," which appeared in the *New York Times* on August 12, 1972. It concludes: "Hundreds of thousands of Soviet Jews may genuinely want to live in Israel, but many more would still be content to live as Communists—if only they were also permitted to live as Jews." However, the definition of a "good Communist" is one who eschews religious or petty nationalist feelings. At the same time, one often hears it said that "only in Israel can a Jew be a Jew." Such an assertion was made by one hundred

American writers and scholars in mid-1972 in a letter addressed to Soviet President Nikolái Podgórny. It said in part: "We appeal to you equally on behalf of Soviet Jews who are dedicated to perpetuating their heritage and feel they can do this only in Israel." [6]

No doubt this is true for those who desire to preserve the old traditions intact. The late Jewish poet Menahem Boraisha has pointed out, "In the Communist scheme of things, there is no room for Jewish survival." [7] Boraisha, who was a pro-Zionist writer, added: "In order to foster Jewish survival, communism would have to open the gates for all individual and collective ideas and aspirations."

No matter how much the Soviet Union can be criticized for its treatment of Jews, most specialists on the USSR agree that Jews in general benefited from the October Revolution; their position is vastly improved over czarist days. The evil geniuses who guided czarist policy had prepared a harsh program of Russification, and for Jews it came to this: one third were to be converted to Christ, another third would be forced to emigrate, and the remainder would be killed. These were the days of the dreaded pogroms. [8] (Jews were also becoming revolutionaries. For instance, in 1877 the records of one czarist police department listed these convicted "radical propagandists": 279 nobles, 197 sons of priests, 117 sons of high officers, 68 young Jews. —From "A Century of Jewish Life in Russia," ABC-TV, May 12, 1974.)

Except for the part about conversion, one sees a certain rough but eerie similarity in Hitler's treatment of Jews. At the Nuremberg War Crimes Trials, one of Adolf Eichmann's agents, Dieter Wisliceny, spoke about the "three distinct periods of activity affecting Jews." He testified:

> Until 1940 the general policy was to settle the Jewish question in Germany and in areas occupied by Germany by means of a planned

emigration. The second phase, from that time on, was the concentration of all Jews in Poland and in other territories occupied by Germany in the East, by concentration in ghettos. This period lasted approximately until the beginning of 1942. The third period was the so-called final solution of the Jewish question, that is, the planned extermination and destruction of the Jewish race; this period lasted until October 1944, when Himmler gave the order to stop their destruction.[9]

Mark Twain, in 1899, commented that, "The Jew is being legislated out of Russia." Twain was aware that the 5 million Jews who owed allegiance to the czar were ghettoized, disenfranchised, persecuted, and terrorized.[10] The Bolshevik Revolution with its aftermath of counterrevolution drove many Jews to seek protection from the Red Army against the White forces, many of whom were wildly anti-Semitic. Massacre of Jews was widespread. In the Ukraine alone almost one hundred thousand noncombatant Jews were killed, and before the bloodletting—carried out by White leaders Antón Deníkin and Símon Petylúra—was done nearly three hundred thousand Jewish children were orphaned and homeless. One bit of czarist mischief dealt with a forgery. In 1903 in the days of Czar Nicholas II, a band of Russian traditionalists and religious zealots drew up a tract called the "Protocols of the Elders of Zion." It alleged that Jews—traditional scapegoats—had an international design to undermine and then dominate Christian civilization. Many Christians in the West quickly recognized it as a gross forgery, but it was widely circulated in Europe and the United States. Even as recently as 1972, the forgery appeared in a newly published edition in Tokyo.

With the toppling of the czar, Jews played an important role in the formation of the new Bolshevik regime and later contributed to the victory over the Nazis. (In World War II, for example, more than forty Soviet generals had Jewish backgrounds.) [11]

Lenin, who unlike Stalin never had any prejudices

toward Jews, was as far back as 1913 attacking nationalism, including a czarist scheme to nationalize Jewish schools. Lenin spoke in opposition to setting up special Jewish schools, which, in effect, meant segregation of Jews. Lenin said: "The most harmful feature in our political life generally, apart from the oppression and persecution of the Jews, is the striving to fan the flames of nationalism, to segregate the nationalities in the streets one from another, to increase their estrangement, to separate their schools." [12] Curiously, Lenin's revolutionary colleague Leon Trotsky could be quite sensitive about his Jewish origins. Trotsky tells us in his autobiography that when Lenin offered him the post of Commissariat of the Interior, he (Trotsky) brought up his Jewish birth, saying that it might be used as a weapon in the hands of their enemies. Lenin was startled.

> LENIN: We are having a great international revolution. Of what importance are such trifles?
> TROTSKY: No doubt the revolution is great but there are still a good many fools left.
> LENIN: But surely we don't keep step with fools.

That is how Trotsky recalled it. Since he persisted, Lenin finally offered him a different job.[13]

By contrast to Lenin, Stalin appeared to have some coarse, peasant prejudices toward Jews. His daughter, Svetlana Alliluyeva, says that Stalin was vexed when his son, Yakov, took a Jewish wife and, later, was chagrined when Svetlana married a Jew during World War II.[14] In the so-called Doctors' Plot of 1952–53, Stalin suspected that a clique of Kremlin physicians, many of them Jews, had plotted to kill off his top-ranking military and political leaders. After Stalin's death it was revealed that the charges against the doctors had been falsified and much of the testimony obtained by torture. All of the doctors survived and were "rehabilitated." Solzhenitsyn has suggested in *The*

Gulag Archipelago that before Stalin's death the dictator had in mind a fantastic impromptu pogrom against Jews, that included staging public executions on Red Square to whip up the anti-Semitic frenzy of the crowds preparatory to wholesale exile of Soviet Jews to Siberia. The idea of the purported exile is not a new revelation; however, the part about the pogrom appears to be a macabre twist to the story, which may or may not be true. Khrushchév in his 1956 anti-Stalin speech said that in addition to actual massive deportation of smaller national groups from their native places, Stalin wanted to deport all the Ukrainians but didn't do it "only because there were too many of them. . . ." [15] Therefore, although the above reference to the pogrom seems ideologically false—anti-Semitism runs counter to basic Marxist-Leninist principles—the mass deportation of Jews was within Stalin's capability.

Stalin did execute countless Jewish artists and intellectuals, and most if not all of them were "rehabilitated," restored formally to their previous reputations, after his death.

Solomón Mikhóels, an actor and director, died by mysterious circumstances in January 1948 while on a trip to Minsk. One report said he was fatally injured in an automobile accident while another said he was brutally killed by hooligans. But there are other reports that say the "accident" was planned with the approval of Stalin. Mikhóels had been head of the Moscow State Jewish Theater, which was closed down about a year after his death. Even Stalin admired his performances, such as his portrayal of the king in Shakespeare's *King Lear*. Indeed, Mikhóels was awarded the Stalin Prize in 1946. But a few years after his death he was being called a "Jewish bourgeois nationalist." Some observers say that Mikhóels's assassination was the first step in stamping out all Jewish culture and most of the outstanding Jewish writers, actors, and artists in the USSR.

On August 12, 1952 in one supreme outburst of madness, twenty-four Jewish writers and intellectuals were executed on charges of "Jewish nationalism." The dead included Leib Kvitkó, David Hófstein, Itsik Féfer, and Pérets Márkish. Kvitkó wrote many poems for children, which were translated into divers languages. Hófstein wrote poetry in Yiddish, Hebrew, Russian, and Ukrainian. Féfer, a Bolshevik, fought in the civil war of 1917–1920 and had held important posts in the Soviet regime. As with the others, but perhaps stronger in the case of Márkish, there were elements of tragic irony in his career. In 1940 one of his epic poems bore the title "Ode to Stalin." The year before he had received the Order of Lenin for his literary contributions to the USSR. One of his novels, published in the Soviet Union after his death, is full of praise for the regime. But neither the ode nor an epic poem of his running to twenty thousand lines, which also praised Stalin to the hilt, was enough to save Márkish from the executioner.[16]

It is said that with the death of these twenty-four writers, artists, and intellectuals, almost every significant institution of Jewish national life in the USSR disappeared. In 1972 a booklet appeared with English translations of works by the above poets. It was entitled *The Night of the Murdered Poets.*

The establishment of Israel in 1948, viewed as a blessing by hundreds of thousands of displaced Jews in Europe, was looked upon with deep suspicion by the Soviet regime. The Kremlin was fearful that the dormant nationalism of its own Jewish population would be awakened. Stalin, however, immediately offered diplomatic recognition to Israel, while simultaneously cracking down on pro-Israeli sentiment of Soviet Jews. Shortly afterward, Zionist leaders in the West became alarmed at the prospect of 3 million Jews in the USSR gradually disappearing into the womb of communism. These leaders charged that Jews were being "trapped" in Russia and demanded that Stalin halt his persecution of them.[17] Israel, which wanted to increase its population, laid fond eyes on Soviet Jews.

Stalin died in 1953. Only then did some Communists feel safe to speak out. In 1956 the American Communist party expressed concern for Soviet Jews and the liquidation by the Kremlin of Jewish cultural leaders in Eastern Europe when it asked Moscow to explain the physical annihilation of the top Soviet Jewish writers and poets in the 1940s.[18]

There remain some "loose ends" about Iosif Stalin; some paradoxes surround the Georgian dictator. For example, some of his closest associates were of Jewish origin. True, he had ordered many Jews who ranked high in the party and government killed or imprisoned. But his best-known foreign minister, Maksím Litvínov, was a Jew, and during World War II Stalin appointed him Soviet ambassador to Washington. Another Jew was Lázar Kaganóvich, one of Stalin's right-hand men, who was Commissar of Transportation and of Heavy Industry. He survived Stalin and was one of his pallbearers.

At least a part of Stalin's attitude toward Jews may be glimpsed in his essay on "Marxism and the National Question," written back in 1913. It contains a section on the Jewish Bund which, among other things, deals with the question of preserving the "national peculiarities of the Jews." Stalin clearly regarded as harmful to society the exclusiveness of any nationality. He wrote that in the name of "national autonomy" extremes of logic were being used whose net effect was to divide people rather than bring them together.

It is unassailable, on the one hand, that many Jews survived the holocaust because of the existence of the

Soviet state. At the outbreak of World War II in 1939 the Soviets opened their borders to approximately one million Jewish refugees from Poland, which Hitler had invaded. On the other hand, Stalin reportedly did some dirty work: he handed over to Hitler, with whom he had signed a nonaggression pact in August 1939, a number of German Jewish Communists who had taken refuge in the USSR.

Some Zionist Jewish sources frankly give credit to Stalinist Russia for helping its Jewish population. Thus, the pro-Israeli writer Menahem Boraisha, writing in 1949, when relations between Israel and the USSR had not yet reached their nadir, said: "It should be remembered that the Soviet government had approached the Jewish problem with the most sincere and honest intention to solve it. It spared no land, no funds, no efforts, in its attempt to build and maintain a 'Jewish nationality' within its framework." Presumably what Boraisha had in mind was the history-making experiment of setting up a primarily Jewish agricultural region in the Soviet Union. This was done between 1928 and 1929 at Birobidzhán, in the Soviet Far East, not far from the city of Khabárovsk. Six years later a Jewish autonomous region was established. But, in the minds of many Jews, Birobidzhán represented a "historic void" compared with Palestine. At any rate, only about thirty thousand Jews settled in Birobidzhán, making up a minority of the population there. Indeed, eleven years after the idea was heralded, with trumpets and banners flying, the so-called Jewish nation on Soviet soil contained less than 1 percent of all the Jews in the Soviet Union, or below thirty thousand.[19]

If Birobidzhán was off the beaten track, it was not exempt from Stalin's campaign against emphasis on Jewish nationality—rather than a common Soviet identity—and any evocation of affinity for Israel. Between 1949 and 1950 it was reported that many of the local

Birobidzháni Jewish Communist leaders were purged, being accused of chauvinism, and dismissed from their jobs. There was also a Stalinist crackdown on the teaching of Jewish culture, and the local Yiddish newspaper was suppressed. Nevertheless, there remains today a Jewish autonomous region at Birobidzhán.

After the death of Stalin, there was considerable easing of anti-Jewish pressures. An example: for years it had been taboo to mention the existence of Jewish martyrs in the Soviet Union killed during the Great Patriotic War, the Soviet name for World War II. Then Yevgény Yevtushenko wrote about Babi Yar, near Kiev, where the Nazis massacred thousands of Jews. The poem won instant popular renown, although there were official objections to some of the wording. (While the poem alludes to anti-Semitism, the Kremlin of course denies that such a practice exists in the USSR.) It is noteworthy that Dmítri Shostakóvich chose to name his Thirteenth Symphony "Babi Yar." Music critic Harold C. Schonberg says the symphony ran into a few snags at its initial performances in the Soviet Union, presumably politically inspired.[20]

Ilyá Ehrenbúrg, a Soviet Jewish writer who, like Borís Pasternak, outlasted the Stalin scourge, once said that the Jewish people outside Israel were nonexistent. He apparently meant that it was not essential for Jews to exist as Jews unless they were Israeli citizens. Ehrenbúrg (who died in 1967) came to this arresting conclusion by equating nationality and Judaism. In his interpretation of the problem, there was no merit whatever in the survival of a fragmented people such as the Jews, particularly since in most advanced countries like America and Britain a man's ancestry hardly mattered.[21]

Could Ehrenbúrg himself be justifiably accused of anti-Semitism?

It is reported that when Soviet leader Alekséi Kosýgin attended a summit meeting with the Czechs in the tense days of the Soviet armed intervention in 1968, he saw somebody he apparently disliked and said: "Why is this Jew from Galicia here?" Another such anecdote concerns Khrushchév. During his American visit in 1959 when he met a Los Angeles official with a Levantine look and a Jewish name, Khrushchév remarked: "But you're not a real American!" Was it anti-Semitism?

In December 1973 an attractive young Jewish girl who had recently emigrated to Israel from the USSR spoke on American television about the acute embarrassment she felt when she was a student in that country. She said that each year at the start of the new school term, all students were required to stand up in class and state their nationality. Hers was Jewish, stamped on her identity card.

Is it a form of anti-Semitism for Jews in the Soviet Union to have to carry around such a document identifying them as Jews? Officially, this practice applies to all nationalities, including Uzbeks, Tatars, Georgians, Latvians, and Lithuanians. A usual Soviet reply is that it is not the state's fault if some Jews are highly sensitive about their birth. But, then, even Soviet officialdom admits that a smattering of anti-Semitism exists in the marketplace. And some charges of anti-Semitism go deeper. Some young Jews assert that bias exists in schooling and concerning job opportunities. (Peter Grose, in his essay "The Kremlin and the Jews," makes an interesting point: that Americans in good conscience, without being hypocrites, ought to find it difficult to attack anti-Semitism in the USSR, socially and professionally, when there is a residue of it in the United States.) [22]

Many studies on Jews in the Soviet Union have been published, some of them pointing to evidences of anti-Semitism. Of course, sometimes what looks to be anti-Semitism is the Soviet policy of promoting atheism, whose ax falls on other religions also. For example, in January 1974 Russian Orthodox monks in the Ukraine protested to Soviet authorities, saying they were being harassed. The monks said their monastery grounds had been taken away, including their kitchen garden.[23]

Paradoxically, under Stalin literally dozens of tracts were published in the USSR on the subject of anti-Semitism, many of them attacking it or attempting to discover its causes. For example, the scholarly work *The Jews in the Soviet Union* by Solomon M. Schwartz (Syracuse University Press, 1951) lists twenty-three writings against anti-Semitism that were published in the four years before 1930. The books include: *Hatred of Jews—Where Does It Come From?—Whom Does It Benefit?*, *Against Anti-Semitism: A Symposium*, *Anti-Semitism on Trial*, and *Anti-Semitism and Anti-Semites.*

Nevertheless, as recently as 1963 a blatantly anti-Semitic book was published in the USSR called *Judaism without Embellishment*, by T. K. Kichko. Moreover, it was not the only anti-Semitic book published that year. Indeed, the Kichko book was so coarse that the authorities were compelled to repudiate it in an article that appeared in *Pravda*, April 4, 1964.

Such political works, however, which are designed for use as pure antireligious propaganda, have little in common with the higher standards of Soviet literature, which must go through a screening process that would weed out obvious nonideological prejudices. (The Kichko book was originally published in Kiev in the Ukrainian language, in a printing of twelve thousand copies.)

It is true that when Soviet literature deals with Jews it invariably conforms to "socialist realism." For example, the novel *In the Homeland* by Soviet writer Tevye Gen tells about a Jewish metallurgical engineer whose family was killed by the Nazis.[24] The war is over, many years have gone by but the hero of the story keeps hoping his daughter is alive, and that he will be able to find her. If so, she would be about twenty years old now. Again and again he looks up many non-Jewish Russian families who risked their own lives to hide and bring up Jewish children during the war. But he does not find his daughter. He remains convinced, though, that unless she landed right in the lap of the Germans, she must have been given refuge by good Russian, Ukrainian, or Byelorussian (White Russian) people, and that his daughter does not even know, perhaps, that they are not her real parents. So he is buoyed up, knowing that his daughter, perhaps alive, is living a good life.

It is, of course, exactly the kind of socialist consciousness the Soviet regime is trying to persuade every citizen to adopt, no matter what his antecedents or nationality. To accomplish this involves the difficult process of breaking down and eliminating the power and attraction of the old standards. Naturally, some Jews resist such a jettisoning of traditions and are therefore susceptible to stimulation from the outside, to the profound annoyance of the authorities. For example, the American writer James Michener quotes a former Soviet Jewish scholar, Professor Mikhaíl Zand, who epitomizes the thinking of some Jewish intellectuals. Zand, who was able to leave the USSR, admits he had a good life with privileges when he lived in the Soviet Union. He even had a small house in the country. But he could not, he said, consent to being what he called a "privileged slave." The reason: "I could not live as a Jew. I could never attain a top position . . . nor travel abroad." [25]

Novelist Borís Pasternak

Novelist Mikhail Sholokhov with Nikíta Khrushchév
Below, physicist Andréi Sakharov and his wife Yelena

Writer Ilyá Ehrenbúrg

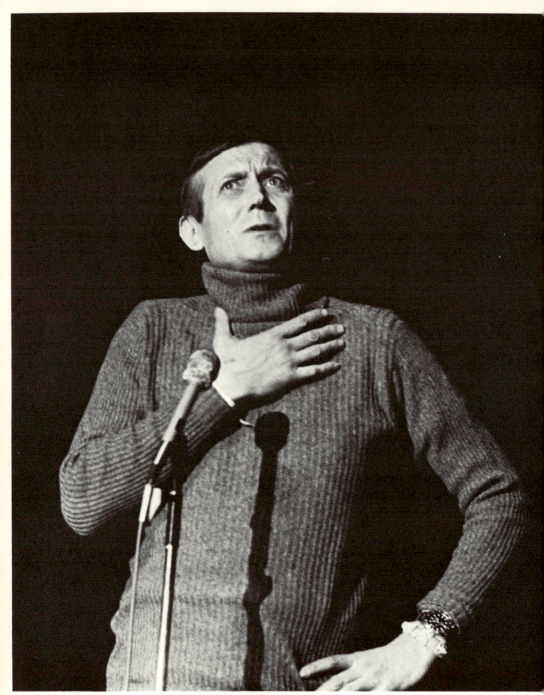

Poet Yevgény Yevtushenko

Writer Aleksándr Solzhenitsyn

Dancer Rudolf Nureyev

Dancers Valery and Galina Panov

5

CONTROVERSY
IN THE BALLET

They [artists] are definitely the elite of Russia.

Clive Barnes,
dance critic of the *New York Times,* 1973

Such individual performers are not always the easiest to fit into organizations, or even into society. But what they have to contribute is unique.

Alexander Bland,
discussing Rudolf Nureyev (*Current Biography,* 1963)

It must be admitted, comrades, that some of our writers and workers in the arts continue to lose their foothold and to stray from the right road.

Nikíta Khrushchév,
On the Arts, 1956

Sir Laurence Olivier, the distinguished actor, was speaking about ballet dancer Valery Panov and his wife, Galina, in April 1974, but he could have been speaking about other artists, past, present, or future: "Anybody in a country he really doesn't like, surely he must be allowed to move. It's as simple as that. And that he wishes to move, that the wish itself should be punishable, is absolutely extraordinary." [1]

And Rudolf Nureyev, perhaps the most famous male ballet dancer in the world, has expressed himself on the same theme in these words: "I feel that everyone has a right to live wherever and however they wish."

What happened was impermissible in the Soviet Union where the politics and conduct of a ballet dancer, as with all artists, are supposed to be impeccable. By asking for official consent to emigrate, the Panovs had in effect repudiated their homeland and scandalized the Kirov Ballet of which they had been star performers.

The prevailing view of the artist in the West is that the artist "belongs to the world," that he therefore has the right to practice his art anywhere, that no one can or ought to stop him. Clive Barnes, the dance critic of the *New York Times,* has said he could not understand why the Soviet authorities persisted in being so stubborn in detaining artists who wished to leave the country. Under Communism, however, art is not a "free commodity" in the Western sense. The Western habit of an artist locking himself up in his castle of "pure art" is intolerable to Soviet orthodoxy. Art, nourished by the Communist state, subsidized by the state, and guided by the state, thus belongs to the state. Perhaps this position on art has reached its most extreme expression in Maoist China where it is drummed into an artist that he has one principal duty: not to fulfill himself or to be "true to art" but to educate the people, to express in artistic form the social and political ideas of the party. The good artist even delays his marriage in the "best interests of the nation." Strange as it may seem, the Soviet Union permits more flexibility for the artist, more freedom for experimentation than China. Yet on occasion a Soviet ballet dancer defects.

Take Rudolf Nureyev, for instance. In 1961 Nureyev was at Le Bourget Airport in Paris, waiting to board a plane for Moscow, presumably to be disciplined for his mutinous ways. (You would hardly find an artist like Nureyev in China.) Nureyev, a rank individualist, can't abide being regulated like a clock or followed wherever he goes. At Le Bourget Nureyev suddenly leaped over a guardrail and defected to the West. About that incident he says simply: "It was time to go." Actually, as he tells it, this acknowledged genius of the ballet didn't know when he left the USSR for France that he would defect.[2] The decision was made on the spot. He was provoked, incensed. And so he leaped over the guardrail. Yet nowadays when he is in a reflective mood, he sometimes thinks about the time when he may even return to the Soviet Union, perhaps when he retires as an active performer in the West. Possibly, if he goes back, he will become a teacher of ballet. ("I hope by then," he says modestly, "I'll have some knowledge to pass on.") Nureyev has also said he would dance in the Soviet Union *now* if he had a guarantee he could leave again.

Valery Panov, also a virtuoso dancer, must be seen in an entirely different context, one that is colored by politics, religion, nationality. Until March 1972 Panov and his wife, Galina, were the star dancers of Leningrad's world-famed Kirov Ballet. Then Panov, who is a Jew, applied for visas to emigrate to Israel with Galina, who is Russian. Any such applications would have angered the authorities, but that such famed dancers wanted to leave the country permanently must have been especially hateful. In the Soviet Union a request to emigrate, particularly from a distinguished artist, must be as repugnant to the regime as an apostate in the eyes of the Catholic church. Panov was dismissed immediately from the Kirov Ballet and condemned as a "hooligan"—a charge the Kremlin often hurls at an individual who is deemed guilty of anti-Soviet behavior. As Clive Barnes has commented, charges of hooliganism are often laid against Soviet Jews who have applied for exit visas but whom the authorities don't for one reason or other wish to release.[3] Later Panov was called a "parasite" because when he was out of work—he was told he would never be allowed to dance again in the USSR—he had to rely on the financial help from friends and well-wishers both at home and abroad. Meanwhile, Galina was demoted and afterward she left the Kirov troupe.

Between Nureyev and Panov, the regime obviously had less antipathy for the former. Objectively speaking, Nureyev had made a clean swift break with the Soviet Union. No central core of politics or ideology was involved. Only temperament. He is neither violently anti-Soviet or anti-Communist. Rather he is a supreme individualist. (But such individualism also constitutes dissent from the system.) Nureyev cannot tolerate being badgered. When this occurs he says he sees yellow lights flicker. Then— if the pressure continues—red lights appear. It is his cue to bolt, to run, to escape. He saw these "red lights" at Le Bourget. The adjectives used to describe Nureyev cover a broad spectrum: difficult, haunted, unique, ingenious, strange, egotistical, stubborn, quixotic. Nureyev candidly admits that he possesses "obstinate egoism." [4]

Anyway, these are hardly the traits that make an obedient citizen.

Rudolf Hametovich Nureyev was born in Siberia in 1938. Like many Russians he has Tatar blood. (The "golden hordes" of the Mongols spent hundreds of years on Russian soil.) He is strong, virile, handsome. He has high cheekbones, his hair is thick and chestnut-colored, and these features, combined with his penetrating eyes, give him a very striking appearance.

Nureyev speaks fluent English and has a fine sense of humor. Once during an interview in New York he was asked if he had any strong political opinions. His puckish reply was typical Nureyev: "Am I supposed to have any?" Withal, he has not cut off all ties with the Soviet Union. On occasion he puts through an international telephone call to his mother and sisters in Leningrad. He says he bears no grudge toward the Soviets. He also says he is not nostalgic over Russia. But if and when he returns, probably the Russians will welcome him back. After all, he is a world-famous artist and he continues to bring credit upon the Soviet school of ballet that fathered him.

The defection of an artist may raise political and social questions about the role of the artist in the country he has defected from. For example, are great artists stifled in an authoritarian society? Put another way, will art in a highly regimented country inevitably lapse into dullness and mediocrity, turning into a kind of factory-built art? The whole issue is enmeshed in a lingering controversy.

Some Western critics, such as Clive Barnes, have declared that the Soviet Union has not produced great art, only great artists. Other critics can hardly agree with this assessment when confronted by the works of such men as Prokófiev, Shostakóvich, Rachmaninov,

Kachaturián, and Sholokhov and Eisenstein, in music, literature, and the cinema. Then, too, perhaps half the world would differ with the other half on a definition of "great art."

For his virtuosity, Valery Panov has received unstinting praise. Barnes has said that technically there is no one in the world to match him. "He is an entirely pure dancer. He has genius." Olivier says of Panov: "He's a character dancer. I'm not an expert, but I would know if technique was all right. I think he's one of the most remarkable people working in that sphere." Again, Barnes says about Panov: "He's a virtuoso character dancer rather than a classic dancer. But he has a technique that you would have to compare with Nureyev. In some ways he jumps higher and moves faster. But he's not a perfect classical technician in the way of Nureyev." Galina, eleven years Panov's junior (Panov was thirty-five years old in 1974), is also highly regarded. In fact, she was being groomed for stardom by the Kirov Ballet, which some dance critics have dubbed the "fountainhead" of all ballet art. Critics were highly complimentary of her performances. Often Galina and Panov danced together. Olivier has called Galina "sweet," "wonderful," "absolutely brilliant," "very beautiful." [5]

After being dismissed from the Kirov Ballet, Panov told a foreign writer that "life without dance for me is death." (Ballet dancers must discipline themselves with daily practice.) An American woman who met the Panovs in 1973, a year after Panov's dismissal, said that one "very sad" thing she observed was that all of Panov's friends were leaving the USSR. They were, she said, mainly Jews who were readily given exit permission. (One joke making the rounds in Leningrad, she said, was that if anybody wanted to get a quickie exit permit he should become friendly with Panov.)

Clive Barnes joined the campaign for the right of the Panovs to leave the Soviet Union. He interpreted the Panov case this way: the Panovs were very prominent in the USSR, Panov had completely rejected the Soviet system, and he was a man with a definite point of view who the regime feared might make anti-Soviet propaganda in the West. According to Barnes, Panov stood as a "great representative of Soviet ballet." He said that Panov would represent Russia in the West "in rather the same way as Nureyev represents Russia in the West." That may be. But when the Panovs arrived in Israel in June, 1974, as the happy recipients of Soviet exit visas, Valery was quoted as saying: "My achievements will be Israel's and Israel's achievements will be mine."

The Soviet view of disaffected artists like Panov may be summed up thus: capitalist countries always try to "purchase" Soviet artists; the clamor outside the USSR for "freedom of emigration" for artists seems on the surface to be humanitarian but really what this cry amounts to is a desire to make propaganda and profit in art. People in the West think many Soviet artists can be seduced by the highest bidder. In reply to charges that it is repressing art, the Soviet Union counters that this is not repression but submission to socialist discipline, an acceptance of political as well as aesthetic guidelines handed down by party experts. In the USSR the ballet, being a state institution, provides ballet lessons to deserving pupils at little or no cost; so the state has a "claim" on a dancer who in turn is supposed to be grateful and dedicated to the regime.

Some Western observers commented early in 1974 that it was a mockery of Soviet democratic pretensions when a police inspector told Panov's wife: "Why do you want to stay with this Jew? We will find you another husband." True, many Russians were not only angry at Panov's emigration request but also had contempt for the man himself, manifesting their feeling in crude anti-Semitism.

As a result of the Panov affair, Soviet-American cultural exchange suffered a temporary setback, as the 1974 American tour of the Kirov Ballet was cancelled on request from the United States side. But previously, political questions had also cancelled a tour by the Bolshoi Ballet. Even in the West there exists a palpable link between art and politics. Moreover, because of the Nureyev and Panov incidents, any Soviet dancer whose life-style or politics was suspect would have little hope of traveling outside Soviet borders.

6

LENIN, STALIN, AND AFTER

Marxism is distinguished from the old utopian socialism precisely by the fact that the latter wanted to build a new society not out of the masses of human material created by bloody, dirty, moneygrubbing, rapacious capitalism, but out of especially virtuous people raised in special greenhouses and hothouses.

Lenin,
Collected Works

A new theory is needed for our new intelligentsia, one teaching the necessity for a cordial attitude toward it, solicitude and respect for it, and cooperation with it in the interests of the working class and the peasantry. . . .

Stalin,
Report to the Eighteenth Party Congress

For centuries, misery and suffering have been the bricks and mortar of Russian history. And many rebels have come forth to challenge the regime. Iván Bolótnikov, Stenka Razin, Kondráty Bulávin, Yemelyán Pugachóv, to name just a few. Lenin's brother Alexander was implicated in an attempt to assassinate Czar Alexander III. The brother was executed in 1887. An official biography says Lenin wondered if his brother had chosen the right path and, deciding against terrorism, he would often say: "That is not the path we shall take." [1]

After the Bolshevik Revolution, Lenin—and later Stalin—had to cope with concerted opposition from within. This crisis was compounded by the presence of foreign armies that entered the country to crush the new regime. Although everything looked desperate (at one time, the Soviet government had lost all of Siberia, Central Asia, the Caucasus, and the Ukraine, with its important production of grain, coal, and steel), the Bolsheviks were victorious.

A word about Lenin: He was the most dominant Slavic personality of modern times and the most important revolutionist of the twentieth century. One can travel through the USSR today and not hear an unkind word about him, although one may catch a few salty remarks about other Soviet leaders. Lenin portraits and statues abound. Lenin looks benign and conciliatory in many of his official portraits, but he was capable of great severity. Lenin helped organize the Cheka, the regime's first political police, which soon showed more efficiency than most of the other government agencies. Walter Duranty in his book *I Write as I Please,* tells a dramatic story of how railroad officials suddenly overcame their lethargy. The country in the early 1920s was in the grip of famine and Felix Dzerzhínsky, the first head of the Cheka, wanted to get grain supplies moving swiftly. At one station where a train was stuck, Dzerzhínsky sent off three or four telegrams to the railway headquarters in Omsk asking for help. No replies came. When he arrived at the headquarters, Dzerzhínsky found the station master and other officials and, proving that he meant business, had them shot on the spot.

On February 23, 1918, *Pravda* published a decree saying that the Cheka could "see no other methods of fighting counterrevolutionaries, spies, speculators, looters, hooligans, saboteurs, and other parasites, than their merciless destruction on the spot." But the Bolsheviks were hurting. Leading Bolsheviks had been assassinated and an attempt was made on Lenin's life in 1918. Dzerzhínsky was blunt about the purpose of the Cheka, forerunner of the KGB: "We stand for organized terror . . . terror is an absolute necessity during times of revolution . . . We terrorize the enemies of the Soviet government in order to stop crime at its inception." Dzerzhínsky admitted that the Chekist terror would continue even if sometimes the innocent suffered with the guilty.[2]

The late Vladímir Mayakóvsky, in his 1924 epic poem about Lenin, which runs seventy-five pages in English translation, said this about the Cheka:

> *Spit in the faces of white dross who tell us*
> *about the Cheka's blood-dousings!*
> *They ought to have seen how, tied by the elbows,*
> *workers were flogged to death by thousands.*
> *Reaction ran amuck. Intellectual bunglers*
> *withdrew, recluses, and became the meekest,*
> *locked themselves in with blinking candles*
> *and smoked incense, the god-damn God-seekers.*[3]

But the Chekist terror seems to have paled before that of the anti-Bolshevik forces. Professor D. F. Fleming in his book *The Cold War and Its Origins* says that "until the Nazis made wholesale murder a scientific business, the campaign of Admiral Aleksándr Kolchák in Siberia resulted in the most gigantic tragedy in all recent times." Japan and the Western Allies helped Kolchák, with American troops fighting in Múrmansk and Archangel.

History buffs may be interested to learn that the architect of the Allied intervention was Winston Churchill, then Britain's war minister. Churchill reported that one single anti-Bolshevik general in the Ukraine, Antón Deníkin, received 250,000 British rifles, thirty tanks, two hundred pieces of artillery, and hundreds of British officers, advisers, and pilots.[4] (Incidentally, George Bernard Shaw said of the British intervention that it was "to our eternal shame.")[5] A year after the revolution, some American newspapers, such as the *New York Times* (December 13, 1918), were urging that United States military forces in the USSR be reinforced. Up until then the Americans had suffered 2,845 casualties.

In 1918 when the future of the Soviet state was very much in doubt, Lenin ordered that "traitors and treason-mongers should be shown no mercy." At that time Lenin issued a decree entitled "The Socialist Fatherland Is in Danger,"[6] which said that "all Soviets and revolutionary organizations are ordered to defend every position to the last drop of blood." All towns and villages near the front lines were to form battalions under supervision of military experts; these battalions were to include all able-bodied members of the bourgeois class, men and women, directed by the Red Guards. Those who resisted, said Lenin, "are to be shot." Editors and journalists were to be mobilized to dig trenches or to do other defense work.

This ironhanded policy worked. Although the civil

war was full of cases of desertion to the anti-Bolshevik side, czarist generals admitted that the Red Army men were capable of enduring greater hardships than the soldiers of the White armies. The reason, said Lenin, was that every mobilized worker or peasant knew what he was fighting for.

Lenin, victim of a terrorist shooting, survived until 1924. In the ensuing power struggle, Stalin triumphed, Trotsky lost. The story of Stalin's youth reads like a handbook for revolutionists. It is full of arrests, imprisonments, exiles, escapes. Between 1902 and 1913 he was arrested and exiled to Siberia six times and escaped five times. A czarist police record said of Stalin: "Very dangerous . . . coarse and brutal . . . disrespectful to the authorities. . . ." [7] Stalin's Siberian exile ended in 1917 when upon the overthrow of the czar all political prisoners were freed.

He was born Iósif Vissariónovich Dzhugashvili in the small village of Gori, Georgia, in 1879. His mother wanted him to become a priest, and as a youth he enrolled in a seminary. But he was outraged by the officials who would spy on the young seminarians, often searching their bunks for illicit literature. It wasn't long before he joined a local band of revolutionaries. Sometimes, to obtain funds for party work Stalin staged bank robberies. Years later, when he came to power, he was surrounded by sychophants who could be easily intimidated.

Stalin was utterly ruthless. It was said that his closest associates didn't know when they were summoned to Stalin's offices whether, when the meeting was over, the waiting limousine would take them straight home or to a prison camp. It is reported that one intellectual and writer who survived the Stalin era, Ilyá Ehrenbúrg, had a bag packed during the days of the purges in case the police came for him. [8] Stalin ordered the execution of many of his closest party comrades. Nikíta Khrushchév has called him "sickly suspicious." Stalin, according to Khrushchév, would look at a man and say: "Why are your eyes so shifty today?" Or "Why are you turning so much today and avoiding to look me directly in the eyes?" He saw enemies everywhere. As a result, Stalin demanded absolute submission to his opinion. Said Khrushchév: "Whoever opposed this concept or tried to prove his viewpoint . . . was doomed to removal from the leading collective and . . . moral and physical annihilation." [9]

Systematically, Stalin killed off the opposition, sometimes by means of sensational purge trials replete with "confessions." Moreover, millions of kulaks, or well-to-do peasants, were starved to death or transported elsewhere due to the forced collectivization of agriculture under Stalin. A few experts have pointed out numerous errors in the trial records; others have suggested that the defendants were hypnotized or drugged in addition to being tortured. Some facts are indisputable: a commission of inquiry set up after Stalin's death concluded that many of the documents had been fabricated and testimonies falsified, resulting in the deaths of many innocent people. The commission said that often the victims, no longer able to withstand barbaric torture, charged themselves with all kinds of crimes, even unlikely ones. Khrushchév reported (in his anti-Stalin speech to the Twentieth Party Congress) that "of 139 members and candidates of the Party's Central Committee who were elected at the Seventeenth Congress, ninety-eight persons, that is, 70 percent, were arrested and shot—mostly in 1937–1938." The commission also found that 1,108 of the total 1,966 voting or advisory members of the Seventeenth Congress were arrested on charges of antirevolutionary crimes.

Stalin believed that "the closer we are to socialism the more enemies we will have." Khrushchév reported that under Stalin the secret police prepared lists of persons whose sentences were drawn up in advance. There were 383 such lists in the 1937–1938 period containing the names of many thousands of party, government, Komsomol (youth organization), army, and industrial workers. Stalin approved these lists. After his death many thousands were rehabilitated, a great number of them posthumously. For example, Yan E. Rudzuták, formerly a commissar for communications, who was in the upper echelon of the party apparatus, "confessed" to antiregime acts but retracted his confession in court and asked that he be permitted to write to the Central Committee of the party. This request was ignored, sentence of death was passed in twenty minutes, and he was shot. He was rehabilitated posthumously. Róbert I. Eikhe, who was a member of the Central Committee of the Communist party, was arrested and under torture signed a confession that he had joined an anti-Stalin organization. He denied his guilt but was shot in 1940. He too was posthumously rehabilitated. In the so-called Doctors' Plot of 1952–1953, Stalin is reported by Khrushchév to have told his chief of state security: "If you do not obtain confessions from the doctors we will shorten you by a head." A number of persons who wished to protest the treachery of Stalin's secret police chief, Lavrénty P. Béria, were shot without any trial. At least one man, Grigóry K. Ordzhonikídze, a foe of Béria, was, Khrushchév said, "forced to shoot himself." [10]

Artists, writers, and poets were particularly vulnerable under Stalin. Sometimes they were admonished and cast into the shadows; but many who were not so lucky were exiled to Siberia or shot. An unusual story concerns Aleksándr Dovzhénko, a film director and writer, and Stalin Prize winner. His films *Arsenal* and *Earth* brought fame but also criticism. Then Dovzhénko wrote a film story about the Nazi invasion of the Ukraine and incurred the anger of Stalin and Béria, who called him a "nationalist," a dirty word in the Communist lexicon. Apparently, his portrayal of Soviet soldiers in retreat was considered anti-Soviet and he was highly condemned and threatened with punishment. But Dovzhénko was not one to be cowed. He wrote Stalin a brave letter in which he denied he was a nationalist and went so far as to berate Stalin for sullying his name. Said Dovzhénko: "I am a part of the people, I am nevertheless greater than you. . . . Since I am very small, I forgive you your smallness and malice, for you are imperfect, even though people pray to you. God exists. But his name is chance." Dovzhénko was lucky enough to live out his life and died a few years after Stalin's death. Other artists like Ósip Mandelshtám had a different fate. Mandelshtám, a highly talented poet, who was critical of Stalin, was sent to prison in the mid-1930s. (Borís Pasternak is said to have made an appeal in his behalf.) The poet was then given a period of exile on conspiracy charges. He attempted suicide, was released briefly, was rearrested and sentenced to forced labor in the Soviet Far East although he was a sick man. He lived a miserable life, was ill much of the time, and died before World War II, at the Vladivostok prison transit camp.

Brooks Atkinson, a Soviet expert and former drama critic for the *New York Times,* says that in the thirties the USSR began to subject artists, including such talented directors as Konstantín Stanislávsky, Vsévolod Meyerhóld, and Aleksándr Taírov, to stricter control. These and others were criticized; indeed, Meyerhóld, in conflict with the authorities, was arrested in 1939 and died in a prison camp. Atkinson says that the harsh controls "succeeded in debasing a glorious, dynamic theater into a dull, spiritless propaganda machine." In his words, art was reduced to public relations.[11]

Others who ended their lives in Stalin's prison camps included writers Borís Pilnyák, Artyóm Vesyóly, Brúno-Viktor Yasénsky, and Isáak Bábel. Many others were simply shot. Some, like poet Ánna Akhmátova and novelist-poet Borís Pasternak, were often pilloried in the 1940s and 1950s. De-Stalinization meant the easing of extreme repression of writers and intellectuals. But it did not mean the regime would cease being tough toward those it considered to be swerving from the correct socialist path.

Prominent writers who survived the Stalin paranoia included Borís Pasternak, Ilyá Ehrenbúrg, and Konstantin Símonov. After Stalin died Pasternak got into hot water with the regime despite the period of relative liberalization. Found especially objectionable by the regime was Pasternak's *Doctor Zhivago*. The *Literaturnaya Gazeta* said it was an "artistically squalid, malicious work replete with hatred of socialism." Pasternak was ridiculed as a "through and through bourgeois reactionary" by *Pravda*. He was called a "hermit crab" because he lived quietly in the writers' colony outside Moscow, forsaking the hustle and bustle of ordinary Soviet life. When Pasternak submitted the manuscript of *Doctor Zhivago* to *Novy Mir* for publication, the editors rejected it. A letter of rejection said: "The spirit of your novel is that of nonacceptance of the Socialist Revolution." The editors added: "The general tenor of your novel is that the October Revolution, the civil war, and the social transformations involved did not give the people anything but suffering and destroyed the Russian intelligentsia, physically and morally." [12]

Although Pasternak was awarded the Nobel Prize, he refused it. Actually, his critics were calling for his banishment to the West. To forestall such an eventuality, he sent a telegram to the Nobel committee and also a note of apology to Chairman Khrushchév. Pasternak's telegram said: "In view of the meaning given to this honor in the community to which I belong I should abstain from the undeserved prize that has been awarded to me. Do not meet my voluntary refusal with ill will." Referring to demands that he be banished, he told Khrushchév: "I am tied to Russia by birth, by life, and by work. I cannot imagine my fate separate from and outside of Russia." And he added that "leaving my homeland would equal death for me." No action was taken against Pasternak and he died in his homeland in 1960.

In attacking Pasternak, the authorities were heeding the ideas set forth in the popular novel *The Yershov Brothers*, by the late Vsevolod Kochetov, which makes the point that it is better to exaggerate danger than to underestimate it. The book portrays disloyal artists, writers, scientists, and students, motivated by base qualities, who have no patriotism for their country and who hate the Communist party. Moreover, they stimulate dissension and disloyalty among nonintellectuals.

Probably the high-water mark of post-Stalin liberalization occurred in 1962. In that year Yevtushenko's poem "Stalin's Heirs" was published in *Pravda,* on October 21. Shortly after, Solzhenitsyn's *One Day in the Life of Ivan Denisovich* appeared. After that there was a retrogression, but never back to the Stalinist extremes.

Isaac Deutscher, author of a monumental biography of Stalin, comments that Stalin found the country using wooden plows and left it with atomic piles. (The first Soviet atomic bomb was tested August 29, 1949;

its first hydrogen bomb four years later.) At the beginning of the twentieth century three quarters of all Russians were illiterate. Today all Russians are literate and they rate high among those people on earth who read extensively. Russia was so backward even in 1931 that Stalin could make the following comment: "The Soviet Union is fifty or one hundred years behind the advanced countries. We must make good this distance in ten years. Either we do it or they crush us." [13] Stalin's foresight was amazing. In 1941 the Germans were at the gates of Moscow and Leningrad. But by then the USSR had made a tremendous leap in industrial and military power. For this purpose, the Soviets had used their own brains plus those of foreigners. In the 1930s (as well as the 1920s) the Soviet Union hired foreign managers and engineers, many of them Americans, to help build up Soviet industry. Today the Soviet Union is one of the world's greatest industrial powers, second only to the United States. Soviet space triumphs are impressive. The USSR was first to loft an artificial satellite (Sputnik I, October 4, 1957), first to photograph the hidden side of the moon, first to put a man into space (Yúry Gagárin), the first and only country to put a woman into space (Valentina Tereshkova), first to have a man walk in space. (Of course, the United States is the first and only country to land men on the moon.)

Soviet industrial production, increasing rapidly, is said to have risen to about two thirds of America's. Moreover, the US-USSR economic gap appears to be shrinking. Soviet power production also is expanding swiftly. Two of the world's largest hydroelectric power stations are located at Bratsk and Krasnoyársk, both in Siberia. Some energy facts: the Soviets claim they have made the "discovery of the century" at Tyumén and Tomsk, meaning they believe they have found the world's largest deposits of oil and gas. Already, the Russians say, they have discovered the world's biggest gas field, between the Urals and the powerful Yenisei River.[14]

Still, however, the standard of living of the ordinary Soviet worker is several notches below his American counterpart, although the Soviet worker would retort that he enjoys job security, has an annual paid vacation, and doesn't have to worry about inflation. (Nasty shortages in some necessary commodities, yes.) But perhaps a truer comparison is to pit today's Soviet worker against his father or grandfather; this is where undeniable progress lies. Today, Ivan can look forward—and not too many years from now—to owning a car, living in a comfortable apartment, and tinkering with fancy electronic gadgets. Many Soviet families already have a small house in the country, called a dacha. The average Soviet man is frugal, hard-working, and appears to be a loyal supporter of the Communist system, even when it represses intellectuals. Perhaps this is inevitable: after all, his ideas come from the newspapers and radio and television. They are of course controlled by the party or government. In any case, the life of most Soviet intellectuals is far removed from that of the ordinary worker.

Anyone who has visited the USSR has praise for its emphasis on education and culture. Russian scholar Paul W. Blackstock says the Soviet students actually read more English and American (and French and German) literature than American students.[15] Even waitresses in the USSR are avid readers. For example, while traveling on the Trans-Siberian Railway, I was surprised to find that the waitresses in the dining car had read works by Ernest Hemingway, Upton Sinclair, and Jack London, in addition to novels by Turgénev, Tolstoy, Dostoyévsky, and Gorky. Soviet authorities assert they have done better by Western authors than the West has done by Russian. A Soviet newspaper declares that even during the height of the "cold war" 6,305 books by American authors were published in the USSR. Most of these were Soviet-favored authors like Theodore Dreiser, Mark Twain, O. Henry, Hemingway, and Jack London. Hedrick Smith reported, however, that there have been fewer translations of American and other writers in the 1970s than in the sixties. Recent translations have included Kurt Vonnegut's *Slaughterhouse Five* and Arthur Hailey's *Airport*.[16]

The Soviet Union has long been concentrating efforts on scientific education and each year the USSR graduates more engineers than America. The Soviets proudly state they have five thousand scientific research institutes, with a total staff of approximately 1 million.[17] Not surprisingly, the Soviets are in a spirited industrial race with America and they hope to overtake the United States by the twenty-first century or before.

7

DÉTENTE AND
DISSENT

I want to see a human détente.

Senator Henry M. Jackson,
interview, 1974

Some persons look at the business community and
say we are only interested in making profits. I have
two children, one 5 and one 7 years old, and I
fought in World War II out in the Pacific in New
Guinea and the Philippines, and I don't want my
children to have to go to war like I did. I don't want
any more Vietnams. I don't want World War III.
And to me the only way that you prevent another
Vietnam and another world war is to continue with
détente, you continue with trade, and you continue
down any avenue whether it's exchange of students,
whether it's exchange of tourism, and no one (I've
heard) has proposed that the United States take
down its military guard.

Donald M. Kendall,
chairman of Pepsico, and member of the US-USSR
Trade and Economic Council, 1974

While I sympathize deeply with the plight of the dissidents and minorities in the USSR, I cannot concur
in the approach of the physicist [Dr. Sakharov] who
said there can be no détente without democracy or
the novelist Solzhenitsyn who said that "mankind's
sole salvation lies in everyone making everything his
business."

Senator William Fulbright,
from a speech delivered in October 1973

Perceptive observers detect considerable irony in the way American liberals look at détente with the Russians. In the 1950s the left-wing sympathies of many liberals exposed them to charges of being "soft on Communism." Now some two decades later, many liberals are among the vanguard of those who doubt the wisdom of Soviet-American détente. Their argument runs this way: that détente plus expanded trade and granting "most-favored-nation status" (equality with other U.S. trading partners) to Moscow puts a stamp of respectability on Soviet internal repression. Détente, they say, lays Americans open to accusations that they are callous and indifferent to the plight of Soviet intellectuals, including Jews who are denied permission to emigrate. As a result, many American liberals plus diehard conservatives have demanded that Washington offer détente only in return for concessions from the Russians, mainly on the freedom of emigration of Jews and others who wish to leave the Soviet Union, and freedom for dissenting intellectuals.

There is an additional irony in the momentum toward détente. Two decades ago the "Wall Street bankers" and other American businessmen saw the idea of negotiating with communists as the next thing to treason. Then, the "best solution" for communism was its extirpation. Today the picture is entirely changed and some of the biggest names in American industry and banking are not only strong supporters of détente but they also favor a major expansion of trade with the Soviet Union, including providing U.S. technological and financial help for developing Soviet natural resources, especially oil and gas. Indeed, the US-USSR Trade and Economic Council, a non-governmental body, includes David Rockefeller, chairman of the Chase Manhattan Bank, A. W. Clausen, president of the Bank of America, and the heads of General Motors, IBM, Kaiser Industries, Pullman, Pepsico, and others.

Many persons applaud this change, which is in line with Nixon administration policy, and members of Congress like Senators Mike Mansfield and William Fulbright have supported such overtures to the Soviets. World peace, say many Americans, demands it. Nevertheless, opposition to détente remains formidable; there is considerable controversy on all the issues surrounding détente. There are liberals as well as conservatives who fear détente; or they insist that encouragement of more freedom and opportunity for dissent in the USSR should be a chief objective of the negotiating process with the Kremlin. Soviet intellectuals like Dr. Sakharov and the exiled novelist Solzhenitsyn have subscribed more or less to this thinking. Professor Marshall Goldman, an associate at the Russian Research Center at Harvard University, has said such pressure is necessary; that the United States should enter into some kind of bargaining arrangement with the Soviets concerning the human side of Soviet life.[1] If not, he said, the United States will be "disgraced." And he even went so far as to say that if no conditions are raised then America must assume some of the responsibility for the continuation of tyranny inside the Soviet Union. According to this view the United States's pursuit of détente makes it easier for the USSR to keep its grip on its own restless intellectuals. Professor Goldman has told the author that an increase in Soviet-American trade does not necessarily lead to an improvement in political ties. But Goldman, in an appearance before the Senate Banking Committee early in 1974, argued that the United States Congress—in view of improvements in the Soviet economic picture and a mutual desire for world trade liberalization—could no longer be unreasonable in withholding concessions wanted by the Russians in exchange for trade and credits.

Another widely held view is that the Soviets crave détente and expanded trade much more than the Americans; that the Kremlin needs trade and technological help from the United States to assist its economic development plans over the next ten or fifteen years, and that hence the Soviets have more to gain than Americans from détente and expanded trade.

Senator Henry M. Jackson, who urges the United States to take a "critical look" at détente, thinks the United States may greatly strengthen the Russians and disadvantage America economically by one-sided trade deals; that Washington may give away more than it safely can or should in arms negotiations, and that it may overlook the cries for liberty and human rights behind Soviet borders. Jackson was one of the principal authors of a trade bill that would deny most-favored-nation trading status and Export-Import Bank credits and credit guarantees to the Soviet Union until it lifted all bars on emigration.

On the other hand, some experts on the USSR, such as Robert Kleiman, a member of the editorial board of the *New York Times,* and former correspondent in Europe, believes the Russians are not going to risk a "brain drain" to the West—through free emigration—and the possibility of losing many doctors, engineers, and scientists to higher wages and the luxuries obtainable in the West.[2] Moreover, Soviet dissident historian Roy Medvédev contends that the tactic of using strong pressure on the Kremlin in this area is unrealistic. Senator William Fulbright, chairman of the Senate Foreign Relations Committee, thinks that the supporters of détente-with-conditions are calling for nothing less than a "revamping of the Soviet system, a dismantling of a Soviet police state apparatus going back half a century under the Communists and a thousand years before that under the czars." This is, Fulbright says, "a worthy sentiment but I submit it is a tall order." [3] Donald M. Kendall, chairman of Pepsico, who has been to the Soviet Union a dozen or more times on business, is quite blunt: "I don't think the Congress can legislate social changes in other countries." [4] Kendall believes there is no other way to obtain a so-called human détente with the Soviets except through trade and quiet diplomacy, that it is not only the best method but that unless the Kremlin is treated as an equal in matters of trade, there will be little room for friendly persuasion.

Marshall D. Shulman, director of the Russian Institute at Columbia University, while critical of Soviet violations of human rights, believes that in the long run the interests of human rights in the USSR will best be served by a prolonged era of reduced tensions—in a word, détente—between the two superpowers, although he admits, as an immediate effect, the tightening of controls by that country's police apparatus.

The U.S. Department of Commerce has been encouraging American businessmen to approach the USSR, telling them that not only are politics and trade separate categories but also that Americans *can* trust the Russians. Sources close to the department point out that Moscow, for its part, trades with countries whose politics it abhors, like Greece and Spain with their right-wing governments; and, moreover, they say that the United States must realize that it is in stiff competition with Japan and other advanced nations for world trade, including the Soviet market. Some American companies are already interested in aiding the development of oil and gas fields in Siberia; others are entering into agreements with the Russians to provide them with industrial plants and technology. One

U.S. oilman, Dr. Armand Hammer, was even reported to have offered to build a golf course in the USSR.[5] Dr. Hammer has trade connections with the Russians going back more than fifty years, including several meetings with Lenin. He is persuasive on the subject of future Soviet-American friendship. On June 17, 1974, he said in an NBC-TV interview: "If you establish good trading relations with people I think it's more apt to lead to friendly relations, especially if there's a mutual need for each other. For instance, if some of these [billion dollar] transactions which we're discussing with the Soviets, like the twenty-year fertilizer deal, [are concluded] they're going to need us for twenty years, we're going to need them for twenty years."

Are the Soviets good credit risks? For those who worry whether they will get their money back, a former Assistant U.S. Secretary of Commerce, Harold Scott, says that since World War I the Soviet credit record has been "impeccable."[6] He has described as "untarnished" the Soviet record vis-à-vis the United States in fulfillment of economic agreements. Given the size of the Soviet economy, Scott says the Americans can look forward to a maximum of US-USSR trade of between $30 billion and $35 billion, which would be almost half of America's total trade. Here is where the critics demur. They have two main arguments: one, that large-size trade with the Russians is a will-o'-the-wisp because Soviet oil and gas reserves are "unproven"; two, that American trade and investments, for example in oil exploration, will be dependent on the whim of the Russians. The Soviet reply is that Soviet sincerity can be measured by the large personal commitment to détente by Communist party secretary Leonid Brezhnev; that his prestige is staked on the success of this policy both at home and abroad. In addition, the Soviets say they have long-term trade agreements in mind that would create an interdependence that the Kremlin would not wish to see destroyed.

Does trade help the Soviets more than it does Americans? Trade expert Harold Scott believes it is very important for the United States to "energize" its domestic economy, and that world trade is one of the best ways to accomplish it. He asserts that projects worth $100 billion are being investigated by the Russians for procurement outside that country. And, says Scott, even if a small fraction of these projects comes to fruition, it would result in substantial American exports to the Soviet Union.

Donald M. Kendall has great expectations for American-Soviet trade—if the United States becomes actively involved in the development of Soviet natural resources, principally in Siberia. If this happens, he says the USSR can become an "equal partner" of America in the realm of trade.

Supporters of détente and increased trade with the Soviet Union point to some positive results: US-USSR trade has risen to 1.4 billion (in 1973) and the Kremlin has eased its jamming of Western radio broadcasts (including the Voice of America) to the Soviet Union. Moreover, the Soviets themselves admit that the October 1973 Middle East war could have been far worse if there had not been US-USSR consultations. Thus, in November 1973 a senior Soviet adviser on American affairs, Georgi A. Arbatov, conceded that a general improvement in Soviet-American relations had prevented a "dangerous confrontation" in the Middle East between the two superpowers. Moreover, this improvement had made possible a quick cease-fire. Arbatov, director of the prestigious USA Institute, made his remarks in a speech celebrating the fortieth anniversary of US-USSR diplomatic relations.[7]

W. Averell Harriman, a former American ambassador to the Soviet Union who has had business contacts with the Russians that span more than fifty years, told the author he opposes the sale of such things as the most complex computers to the Soviets (because of their special importance to military uses) but he was categorical about the negative results in the past of keeping American trade with Moscow to a minimum. "We have achieved nothing by not trading and have lost useful business," he said, adding that the Soviets had gotten almost everything they could from the United States from other nations. On Soviet-American relations, Harriman said the following: "I am in favor of détente and trade with the Soviets as far as they permit it to develop. I think it is to our interest to get away from confrontation and reach agreements in our mutual interests wherever possible." The word "détente" means relaxing of tensions, said Harriman. "Obviously, this is desirable."

Given the multiplicity of experts on the Soviet Union, it is difficult to get general agreement on many subjects, especially that of civil rights. However, it appears to be generally recognized that changes in Soviet internal policy, such as the rights of citizens, will not come mainly from outside pressure but rather from within Soviet society itself. Even the most ardent critics of détente admit that in the past twenty years opposition and dissent inside the Soviet Union has been rising. Dissent is more open. There have been demonstrations in front of the Foreign Ministry, people have stood up for their rights, underground literature has been circulated. As one Soviet specialist has put it, people who have been arrested have even pleaded "not guilty," a far cry from the old days when forced confessions were the rule. Repression persists; but dissidents are not dealt with as harshly as they were two decades ago. Emigration controls have been loosened.

Critics of détente point out that interdependence does not prevent the danger of hostilities; that in 1941, for instance, Japan was America's best customer for many commodities. Also, that prior to World War II Germany and France were the best of trading partners. But there is a big difference today: the Bomb. In the nuclear age, says Senator Mike Mansfield, "there is no alternative to détente." Also, before World War II summitry among the great powers was impotent and could not prevent aggression on a grand scale by outlaw nations. Today, few would deny that summit meetings between the US and the USSR (and other nations) lead to positive reductions in world tension, and also to the probability of lasting peace.

According to the Nixon-Kissinger diplomacy, the United States should attempt to create, in the words of Robert Kleiman, "a web of common interests" with the Soviet Union which would lead both sides to use caution in any world crisis that might lead to war, especially nuclear war. Such interests include the limitation on strategic weapons. William Fulbright is categorical on the issue of détente: "We have to get along with the Russians because in matters of world peace we cannot get along without them." In a speech delivered at the "Pacem in Terris III" convocation in October 1973, Fulbright compared the US and USSR to travelers in the same desert who must cooperate with each other. He said: "In the desert it is not ideology that counts but food and water, the food and water of trade, of arms control, of political cooperation, and of cultural exchange."

At the same time Fulbright wondered why some

Americans were so distressed about denial of civil
rights in the USSR when the United States gives large
amounts of material assistance to many non-Communist dictatorships "who also mistreat their citizens."
"Why," he asked, "do we suddenly require measures
for democracy in the Soviet Union as the price for our
trade?" Fulbright mentioned that Chile, Brazil, and
Greece were vulnerable and should be responsible to
American pressures, but he said none of them was
quite as essential a partner for the maintenance of
world peace as the Soviet Union. Along these lines,
U.S. Secretary of State Henry A. Kissinger recently
said that for half a century the United States objected
to Communist efforts to change the domestic struc-
tures of other countries, and that for the past decade
or more it had sought to ease the risks produced by
competing ideologies. In sum, he wondered if Americans would be taking a backward step by insisting on
Soviet "domestic compatibility" as a condition for progress.[8]

The following excerpt involving détente and civil
rights from President Richard Nixon's news confer-
ence of February 25, 1974 illustrates official policy:

QUESTION: Mr. President, what is your personal reaction to the
expulsion from the Soviet Union of Aleksándr Solzhenitsyn, and
will it in any way affect our policy of détente?

PRESIDENT NIXON: Well, my personal reaction is that I am of
course an admirer of a man who has won a Nobel Prize for literature and one who has also shown, as he has shown, such great courage. Second, as far as our relations with the Soviet are concerned,
if I thought that breaking relations with the Soviet or turning
off our policy of negotiation and turning back to confrontation
would help him or help thousands of others like him in the Soviet
Union, we might do that. On the other hand, I look back to the
years of confrontation and I find that men like him, as a matter of
fact, rather than being sent to the West would have been sent to
Siberia or probably worse. As far as our relations with the Soviet
are concerned, we shall continue to negotiate, recognizing that they
don't like our system or approve of it, and I don't like their system

or approve of it. . . . [It] is essential that both nations, being the superpowers that we are, continue to make progress toward limiting arms, toward avoiding confrontations which might explode into war. . . .

President Gerald R. Ford, realizing the importance of greater East-West exchange, is carrying forward the momentum of Soviet-American relations. W. Averell Harriman has said that the trend in the Soviet Union toward greater freedom of expression, although extremely limited, is going to continue.[9]

NOTES

1
THE AGONY OF DISSENT

1. The American and Soviet political systems are of course poles apart. While the majority of Americans are members of one of two political parties, and during election time especially they attack the opposition with boundless zeal, such dissent is disallowed in the Soviet system.

In the USSR there is only one party, the Communist party (some 14,500,000 persons are members and they are the elite of the country), and the party controls the government and armed forces. No opposition to the party is permitted. Or as Lenin is supposed to have joked: there can be many opposition parties but only on condition that the Communist party has all the power and the others are in jail!

The Soviet government accepts all party decisions, puts them into law, and enforces the law. A Soviet voter thus has one choice: the nominee of the party. If the voter wants, he may pencil out the name of the party's choice. But this is rare. The Communists justify their monopoly by saying that parties represent classes, but as there is only one class—the proletarian—in the USSR, an opposition party is superfluous. Differences of opinion are supposed to be ironed out at the many thousands of local party organizations. The USSR comprises fifteen union republics each of which is governed by a soviet or council. The name "Russia" refers only to the largest of the republics but very often it is used interchangeably, though incorrectly, with Soviet Union.

2. See Dr. Andréi Sakharov's book, *Sakharov Speaks* (New York: Alfred A. Knopf, 1974).

3. Those interested in probing charges that mental hospitals have been used to punish political dissenters may wish to see the book *A Question of*

Madness by the Medvédev brothers; see also Theodore Shabad's article, "Soviet Doctors Assail Criticism," *New York Times*, October 3, 1973.

4. Anatold Shub, "The Escalation of Soviet Dissent—And of Soviet Repression," *New York Times Magazine*, September 10, 1972.

5. "A Letter of Rejection: The Case Against *Doctor Zhivago*," *New York Times Book Review*, December 7, 1958.

6. Hedrick Smith, *New York Times*, February 18, 1974.

7. "Rostropovich Appeals for Solzhenitsyn," *Saturday Review*, November 28, 1970.

8. Associated Press, March 12, 1974.

2

SOLZHENITSYN: FROM MARXIST TO MYSTIC

1. Hans Bjorkegren, *Aleksándr Solzhenitsyn* (New York: Joseph Okpaku, 1972).

2. Aleksándr Solzhenitsyn's *The Gulag Archipelago* (New York: Harper & Row, 1974).

3. Ibid. Some observers compare Stalin's and Hitler's concentration camps. But the Nazi camps were in a class by themselves. See, for instance, the searing documentaries, *Treblinka* by Jean-Francois Steiner (New York: Simon & Schuster, 1967) and *The Theory and Practice of Hell* by Eugene Kogon (New York: Octagon Books, 1972).

4. See Bjorkegren, *op. cit.*

5. See Zhores Medvédev's *Ten Years after Ivan Denisovich* (New York: Alfred A. Knopf, 1973).

6. Anthony Astrachan, "Solzhenitsyn—Who Pays the Price?" *New Republic*, March 2, 1974.

7. Solzhenitsyn's letter to the Fourth Congress of the Union of Soviet Writers, available in *One Day* (Praeger edition) and numerous works on the author.

8. See Leopold Labedz, *Solzhenitsyn: A Documentary Record* (New York: Harper & Row, 1971).

9. Robert G. Kaiser, "Writer Says Dissidents Anger Russians," *New York Post*, January 11, 1974.

10. See Theodore Shabad, "Solzhenitsyn Asks Kremlin to Abandon Communism and Split Up Soviet Union," and Nan Robertson, "A Russian Nationalist Looks to the Past," *New York Times*, March 3, 1974.

11. Hedrick Smith, *New York Times*, April 1, 1974.

12. Harrison E. Salisbury, "A Great Writer Is a Second Government," *The Atlantic*, April 1974. For additional critical analyses of Solzhenitsyn see "The Real Solzhenitsyn" by Jeri Laber, in *Commentary*, May, 1974, and "On Solzhenitsyn in Reverse" by Hans Koning, *New York Times*, June 10, 1974.

3

SAKHAROV: CIVIL RIGHTS CHAMPION

1. From Jay Axelbank's interview with Sakharov, *Newsweek,* Nov. 13, 1972; also see *New York Times,* March 5, 1974.
2. *New York Times,* November 30, 1973 and *New York Post,* November 29, 1973.
3. *Current Biography,* 1971.
4. Hedrick Smith, "The Intolerable Andrei Sakharov," *New York Times Magazine,* November 4, 1973.
5. Ibid. The present writer was also on hand when Sakharov made this disclosure to foreign journalists gathered in the physicist's Moscow apartment, August 21, 1973.
6. *New York Times,* March 5, 1974.
7. Open letter from M. V. Kéldysh, president of the Soviet Academy of Sciences to Philip Handler, president of the American National Academy of Sciences, *New York Times,* October 18, 1973.
8. But a much fuller explanation of Kápitsa and his interest in the dissident problem is contained in Zhores Medvédev's *Ten Years after Ivan Denisovich.*
9. See Solzhenitsyn's letter "Peace and Violence," *New York Times,* September 15, 1973.
10. From Smith's "The Intolerable Andrei Sakharov."
11. *New York Times,* October 22, 1973.
12. "Hired Killers," *New York Times,* October 31, 1973.

4

JEWS IN THE USSR

1. In Isaac Deutscher's *Stalin: A Political Biography* (London: Oxford University Press, 1967).
2. Hedrick Smith, *New York Times,* September 8, 1971.
3. Veniamin Levich, "The Freedom to Leave," *New York Times,* December 17, 1973.
4. Bernard Gwertzman, *New York Times,* October 3, 1973.
5. Bernard Gwertzman, *New York Times,* March 19, 1974.
6. *New York Times,* August 12, 1972.
7. Menahem Boraisha, "Communism and Jewish Survival," *Congress Weekly,* February 21, 1949.
8. James G. Gillespie, *Europe in Perspective* (New York: Harcourt, Brace and Company, 1945).
9. The Trial of German Major War Criminals, Proceedings of the International Military Tribunal Sitting at Nuremberg, Germany, London, 1946, Part 4.
10. Mark Twain, *The Damned Human Race* (New York: Hill and Wang, 1962).

11. William Mandel, *Russia Re-Examined* (New York: Hill and Wang, 1964).
12. V. I. Lenin, *On Youth* (Moscow: Progress Publishers, 1970).
13. From Trotsky's *My Life* (New York: Grosset and Dunlap, 1960).
14. Svetlana Allilúyeva, *Twenty Letters to a Friend* (New York: Harper & Row, 1967).
15. From Nikíta Khrushchév's address to the twentieth Communist Party Congress in Moscow, February 24–25, 1956. Text made public by U.S. State Department.
16. *Encyclopædia Judaica* (New York: Macmillan, 1971).
17. American Jewish Committee, report on February 5, 1953, contained in "Facts on File," February 6–12, 1953.
18. Joseph Clark in *N.Y. Daily Worker,* July 3, 1956.
19. Solomon M. Schwartz, *The Jews in the Soviet Union* (Syracuse: Syracuse University Press, 1951).
20. Harold C. Schonberg's "The World of Music," from *The Soviet Union: The Fifty Years,* 1967, edited by Harrison E. Salisbury.
21. Quoted in Boraisha, "Communism and Jewish Survival."
22. Peter Grose, "The Kremlin and the Jews," from *The Soviet Union: The Fifty Years.* Theodore Shabad reported July 7, 1974 in the *New York Times:* "Manpower statistics recently published in Moscow show that Jews play an even more significant role among senior Soviet science personnel than had been recognized. While making up 1 per cent of the population, Jews account for 14 per cent of scholars with doctoral degrees.

    "The large portion of Jews in the top levels of the Soviet science establishment may help explain the continuing reluctance of the authorities to allow scientists and engineers to leave the country."
23. *New York Times,* February 1, 1974. (Other nationalities are also affected. For example, on February 25, 1974 the Associated Press reported from Moscow that twelve Soviet citizens of German origin were arrested during a demonstration demanding permission to emigrate to West Germany.)
24. From Abraham Gontar, "The Jewish Question," in *The Way Things Are* (Moscow: Novosti Press, 1964).
25. James Michener, "Soviet Jewry: 'We Want Moral Outcry,' " *New York Times,* September 16, 1972.

5

CONTROVERSY IN THE BALLET

1. Sir Laurence Olivier made his remarks in a special NBC-TV program on the Panovs, April 3, 1974.
2. Dick Cavett's interview with Nureyev on ABC-TV, November 1, 1973.
3. Clive Barnes, replying to questions about the Panovs on New York City's Channel 31 television station, December 17, 1973.
4. *Current Biography,* 1963.
5. Lord Olivier in the special television program on the Panovs.

6

LENIN, STALIN, AND AFTER

1. A. I. Ulyanova, "Lenin's Boyhood and Adolescence," a booklet published in English by Progress Publishers, Moscow, 1972. (The author is Lenin's sister.)
2. From E. J. Scott, "The Cheka," in *Readings in Russian History,* vol. II, edited by Sidney Harcave (New York: Thomas Y. Crowell, 1962).
3. Vladímir Mayakóvsky, *Poems* (Moscow: Progress Publishers, 1972).
4. D. F. Fleming, *The Cold War and Its Origins,* vol. I (New York: Doubleday, 1961).
5. George Bernard Shaw, *On the Rocks* (1933). The quotation is from the preface to the play.
6. Lenin, *Collected Works,* vol. 27, pp. 30–33. (Moscow: Progress Publishers).
7. Jack Fishman and J. Bernard Hutton, *The Private Life of Josef Stalin* (London: Hutton, 1962).
8. Harrison E. Salisbury's "Literature: The Right to Write," in *The Soviet Union: The Fifty Years.*
9. Khrushchév's address to the Twentieth Party Congress.
10. Ibid.
11. Brooks Atkinson, *New York Times,* January 12, 1958.
12. "A Letter of Rejection," *New York Times Book Review,* December 7, 1958.
13. J. V. Stalin, "The Tasks of Business Executives," in *A Documentary History of Communism,* vol. II, edited by Robert V. Daniels (New York: Vintage Books, 1960).
14. Georgi Kublitsky, "Siberia, My Native Land," in *Glimpses of Siberia* (Moscow: Progress Publishers, 1972).
15. Paul W. Blackstock, *We Never Make Mistakes* (Columbia, S.C.: University of South Carolina Press, 1963).
16. Hedrick Smith, *New York Times,* October 21, 1973.
17. Novosti Press Agency Year Book, Moscow, 1972.

7

DÉTENTE AND DISSENT

1. Remarks made in a television debate on trade with the Soviet Union, Dec. 13, 1973. Public Broadcasting Service, Channel 13 in New York.
2. Ibid.
3. Senator Fulbright's "Pacem in Terris III" speech, Washington, D.C., October 8, 1973.
4. Round-table discussion on Soviet-American détente, March 3, 1974, on Channel 11, New York.
5. *New York Times,* November 18, 1973.
6. Debate on trade, Channel 13, *op. cit.*

7. "Soviet Concedes Accords with U.S. Averted Confrontation," *New York Times,* November 16, 1973.

8. Kissinger's remarks to the press, February 13, 1974.

9. W. Averell Harriman, "From Stalin to Kosygin: The Myths and the Realities," in *Red Russia: After 50 Years* (New York: A Cowles Book, 1967).

BIBLIOGRAPHY

Allilúyeva, Svetlana. *Twenty Letters to a Friend.* New York: Harper & Row, 1967.

Bjorkegren, Hans. *Aleksándr Solzhenitsyn: A Biography.* New York: Joseph Okpaku, 1972.

Blackstock, Paul W. *We Never Make Mistakes.* Columbia, S.C.: University of South Carolina Press, 1963.

Burg, D., and Feifer, G. *Solzhenitsyn: A Biography.* New York: Stein and Day, 1972.

Conquest, Robert. *The Great Terror: Stalin's Purge of the Thirties.* New York: Macmillan, 1968.

Deutscher, Isaac. *Stalin: A Political Biography.* London: Oxford University Press, 1967.

Dudintsev, Vladimir. *Not by Bread Alone.* New York: E. P. Dutton, 1957.

Duranty, Walter. *I Write as I Please.* New York: World, 1935.

Florinsky, Michael T., Editor. *McGraw-Hill Encyclopedia of Russia and the Soviet Union.* New York: McGraw-Hill, 1961.

Labedz, Leopold, ed. *Solzhenitsyn, A Documentary Record.* New York: Harper & Row, 1971.

Lenin, V. I. *On Youth.* Moscow: Progress Publishers, 1970.

Lyons, Eugene. *Stalin, Czar of All the Russias.* New York: Lippincott, 1940.

Mandel, William. *Russia Re-Examined.* New York: Hill and Wang, 1964.

Medvédev, Roy A. *Let History Judge: The Origins and Consequences of Stalinism.* New York: Alfred A. Knopf, 1971.

Medvédev, Roy A., and Medvédev, Zhores. *A Question of Madness.* New York: Alfred A. Knopf, 1971.

Medvédev, Zhores. *Ten Years after Ivan Denisovich.* New York: Alfred A. Knopf, 1973.

Miller, Wright. *Who Are the Russians?* New York: Taplinger, 1973.

Reve, Karel Van Het. *Dear Comrade: Pavel Litvinov and the Voices of Soviet Citizens in Dissent.* London: Pitman, 1969.

Sakharov, Andréi D. *Progress, Coexistence and Intellectual Freedom.* New York: Norton, 1968.

Salisbury, Harrison E., ed. *The Soviet Union: The Fifty Years.* New York: Harcourt, Brace and World, 1967.

Schwartz, Solomon. *Jews in the Soviet Union.* Syracuse: Syracuse University Press, 1951.

Solzhenitsyn, Aleksándr I. *Cancer Ward.* New York: Dial, 1968.

——. *First Circle.* New York: Harper & Row, 1968.

——. *The Gulag Archipelago, 1918–1956.* New York: Harper & Row, 1974.

——. *The Nobel Lecture on Literature.* New York: Harper & Row, 1972.

——. *One Day in the Life of Ivan Denisovich.* New York: Praeger, 1963.

——. *Stories and Prose Poems.* New York: Farrar, Straus and Giroux, 1971. [Includes "Matryona's House."]

Trotsky, Leon. *My Life.* New York: Grosset and Dunlap, 1960.

Yevtushenko, Yevgény. *A Precocious Autobiography.* New York: E. P. Dutton, 1963.

INDEX

ABOUT
THE AUTHOR

Albert Axelbank has been a writer, teacher, and journalist for more than fifteen years. His articles have appeared in *Harper's, The Nation, The New Republic,* the *New York Times,* the *Montreal Star,* and the *London Economist.* Formerly he taught in the International Division of Sophia University in Tokyo. The author of four previous books, Axelbank has traveled extensively in the Soviet Union and the Mongolian People's Republic.

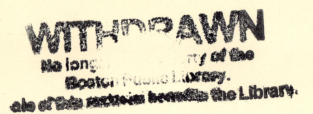